THE
MEANING
OF
HISTORY

ERICH KAHLER

THE MEANING OF HISTORY

Meridian Books

THE WORLD PUBLISHING COMPANY

CLEVELAND AND NEW YORK

A MERIDIAN BOOK

Published by The World Publishing Company
2231 West 110th Street, Cleveland, Ohio 44102
Published simultaneously in Canada by
Nelson, Foster & Scott Ltd.
First Meridian printing 1968
Reprinted by arrangement with George Braziller, Inc.
Copyright © 1964 by Erich Kahler
Library of Congress Catalog Card Number: 64-13416
Printed in the United States of America.

This book was intended to bear the dedication *For and against my friend Ernst H. Kantorowicz,* in testimony to our years of controversial discussion, which only deepened a lifelong affection. He knew of this dedicatory form and accepted it, but he did not live to see what was to be given him. It remains for me sadly to dedicate this paradoxical gift to his memory.

September 1963

Acknowledgments

I wish to express my deeply felt gratitude to my friend, Professor Kimberly Sparks of Princeton University, for his precious advice in putting the final touches to this book.

Unless otherwise indicated, translations are my own.

E. K.

The author wishes to thank the following for permission to reprint the material included in this volume:

COLUMBIA UNIVERSITY PRESS—for selection from Julian H. Franklin, *Jean Bodin and the Sixteenth Century Revolution in the Methodology of Law and History*, 1963.

HARVARD UNIVERSITY PRESS—for selections from Charles H. Haskins, *The Renaissance in the Twelfth Century*, 1927.

Contents

Καθόλου μὲν γὰρ ἔμοιγε δοκοῦσιν οἱ
πεπεισμένοι διὰ τῆς κατὰ μέρος ἱστορίας
μετρίως συνόψεσθαι τὰ ὅλα παραπλήσιόν
τι πάσχειν, ὡς ἂν εἴ τινες ἐμψύχου καὶ
καλοῦ σώματος γεγονότος διερριμμένα τὰ
μέρη θεώμενοι νομίζοιεν ἱκανῶς αὐτόπται
γίνεσθαι τῆς ἐνεργείας αὐτοῦ τοῦ
ζῴου καὶ καλλονῆς. εἰ γάρ τις αὐτίκα μάλα
συνιθεὶς καὶ τέλειον αὖθις ἀπεργασάμενος
τὸ ζῷον τῷ τ' εἴδει καὶ τῇ τῆς ψυχῆς
εὐπρεπείᾳ κἄπειτα πάλιν ἐπιδεικνύοι τοῖς
αὐτοῖς ἐκείνοις, ταχέως ἂν οἶμαι πάντας
αὐτοὺς ὁμολογήσειν διότι καὶ λίαν πολύ τι
τῆς ἀληθείας ἀπελείποντο πρόσθεν καὶ
παραπλήσιοι τοῖς ὀνειρώττουσιν ἦσαν.

(He indeed who believes that by studying isolated histories he
can acquire a fairly just view of history as a whole, is, it seems
to me, much like one who, after having looked at the dissevered
limbs of an animal once alive and beautiful, fancies he has been
as good as an eyewitness of the creature itself in all its action
and grace. For could any one put the creature together on the
spot restoring its form and the comeliness of life and then show
it to the same man, I think he would quickly avow that he was
formerly very far away from truth and more like one in a
dream.)

POLYBIUS
Book I, 4

L'allure principale entraîne avec elle tous les accidents particuliers.

(The principal current of events carries all specific events.)

MONTESQUIEU
Grandeur et décadence des Romains

Or, ce temps véritable est, par nature, un continu. Il est aussi perpétuel changement. De l'antithèse de ces deux attributs viennent les grands problèmes de la recherche historique.

L'incompréhension du présent naît fatalement de l'ignorance du passé. Mais il n'est peut-être pas moins vain de s'épuiser à comprendre le passé, si l'on ne sait rien du présent . . . Car le frémissement de vie humaine, qu'il faudra tout un dur effort d'imagination pour restituer aux vieux textes, est ici directement perceptible à nos sens.

(Now, this real time is, by nature, a continuum. It is also perpetual change. The great problems of the study of history derive from the antithesis of these two attributes.

The failure to comprehend the present arises ineluctably from ignorance of the past. But it is perhaps no less futile to exert oneself in trying to understand the past, if one knows nothing of the present . . . For the pulsation of human life, whose reconstitution of old texts makes extreme demands on the imagination, is here directly accessible to the senses.)

MARC BLOCH
Apologie pour l'Histoire

I

THE
MEANING
OF
MEANING

1

THIS ESSAY WAS CONCEIVED AS A DEFENSE OF HISTORY. An apology is required, since history, or, more specifically, the use of the historical viewpoint for the clarification of problems and phenomena, has widely fallen into disrepute. The Great Books movement is not the only one to exhibit a basic aversion to the historical and evolutional approach. Positivism, Existentialism, the American school of purely descriptive anthropology, the New Criticism, and, especially in Europe, a trend of thought deriving from Nietzsche, all of them reject the historical point of view. In fact, as will be seen later, a whole epochal mood has found its expression in this anti-historical tendency.

Such a general attitude is not a matter of purely academic concern; its effects reach the very core of our cultural condition. To understand this, we only have to compare the periods when people firmly believed in a meaning of history—the Middle Ages and the period of Enlightenment—with our own age in which this belief is thoroughly shaken. Although human beings in those periods were innately no better than they are today, and certainly their material condition was infinitely worse, their faith in history as a road to salvation, or as the ascending road of human progress, afforded them a definite spiritual framework which guided and guarded the minds of the epoch. It gave man support and orientation in life; it provided him with intellectual security and with a no less protective responsibility for the future of his kind. It prevented the individual from falling into that state of utter "shelterlessness"—to use an expression of Karl Jaspers—which made possible those intellectually sanctioned and technologically engineered horrors peculiar to our age.

We cannot revive the spirit of the Middle Ages, we cannot recover the naive optimism of the Enlightenment; nor can we go back to their concepts of history. There is no return to any former stage. Conditions change, and new ideas and designs must be derived from new states of affairs. The meaning of history has become questionable, and so we have to question it. And in doing so, we have to take into account all the experiences, actual and intellectual, that we have undergone to this very day.

I have to begin by resolving a common confusion which holds sway even in so exquisite a mind as R. G. Collingwood's. In his *Idea of History* he writes: "Every historian would agree, I think, that history is a kind of research or enquiry."[1]

History, I would argue, is by no means identical with historiography, or historical research; otherwise these long-established terms would not make any sense. The fact that these terms exist, that we can conceive of a "study of history" gives sufficient evidence that history is to be understood as the happening itself, not the description or

[1] *The Idea of History* (Oxford, 1946), p. 9.

16

investigation of this happening. To be sure, the concepts and representations of history merge with history itself; they themselves become events influencing history, engendering new history. But only in this active and activating capacity does historiography constitute history, not as a separate, theoretical function.

History is happening, a particular kind of happening, and the attendant whirl it generates. Where there is no happening, there is no history. Sheer eternity—as far as it can be imagined at all—ever stable permanence devoid of all change, and that means the void as such, absolute nirvana, has no history. And the opposite, that is, sheer happening, a completely chaotic, casual, kaleidoscopic mélange of events —which is equally unimaginable, for any event has some connection with other events—does not make history either. To become history, events must, first of all, be related to each other, form a chain, a continuous flow. Continuity, coherence is the elementary prerequisite of history, and not only of history, but even of the simplest story.

There is no isolated event. Any event is connected with other events, those which brought it about and those which it brings about. Nor does connection of events in itself make a story, let alone history. To form a story, the *connection* of happenings must have some *substratum,* or focus, something to which it is related, somebody to whom it happens. This something, or somebody, to which, or whom, a connection of events relates, is what gives the plain connection of events an actual, specific *coherence,* what turns it into a story. But such specific coherence is not given of itself, it is given by a perceiving and comprehending mind. It is created as a *concept,* i.e. as a meaning. Thus, to make even a simple story, three factors are indispensable: connection of events, relatedness of this connection to something, or somebody, which gives the events their specific coherence, and finally a comprehending mind which perceives this coherence and creates the concept which means a meaning. What I propose to demonstrate in the following is that the questioning of and questing after a meaning of history both beg the question. There is no story, there is no history without meaning.

Meaning signifies coherence, order, unity of diverse happenings and phenomena, as grasped by a comprehending mind. When we say that something has a meaning we want to indicate that it forms part of something larger, or superior to itself, that it is a link, or a function within a comprehensive whole, that it points to something beyond. Or, that this something represents in itself a consistent whole, a coherent order in which the parts relate to each other and to the whole. Such coordinate wholeness as seen by the mind, such elucidation of a group of phenomena as a coherent order raises these phenomena from the level of mere being—of plainly sensory, incoherently factual perceptibility—to the level of clear comprehensibility; whereby order is established, the existence of order in the world, and again meaning is synonymous with pointing to something beyond.

When we say that an act or an event is meaningful, we understand that it serves some purpose, or explains some other phenomenon; that something is being done for something or somebody else, that it is aimed for instance at making money—certainly the lowest kind of meaning—or at getting position and influence; that it is done for the welfare of our family, for someone we love, for our community, for humanity, for God. When certain personalities—Lincoln, Einstein, Gandhi for instance—carry enhanced meaning for us, this implies not only that these men have devoted their lives to the common good, but that, by the consistency of their striving, by the subordination of all single moves to one dominating idea, or a consistent set of ideas, they have shown life itself as a coherent whole, as an idea that is valid for other lives too, that they have symbolized the life of man, made it into a sign, made it "significant."

Meaning, then, is an indication of something beyond mere existence, either an end and aim, or the notion of form. Hence, two modes of meaning may be distinguished: *meaning as purpose, or goal,* and *meaning as form.* Any action, design, quest, or search carries meaning as purpose, any work of art is meaning as form.

From all this it follows that something has a meaning only *for somebody,* only for the human mind which comprehends[2] it, and by comprehending it actually creates it; he who grasps a meaning for the first time creates *something new;* by his mere act of comprehending he changes the picture of his world and—since this picture involves a reflexive change in his environment—changes his world itself, the reality of his world. And this is precisely how history came into being.[3]

---

[2] "Comprehending" is, in our context, not limited to *rational* comprehension; it designates something more general, of which rational comprehension is only an advanced stage. Comprehension, as it is used here, is rooted in the stem sense of the word: any encompassing and connecting of a variety of data in a mental act, which reveals some latent connection of these data.

[3] For most people meaning is plainly identical with purpose: ideals too are purposes. And to any one who sees meaning solely in purpose, history must today necessarily appear meaningless: absolute ideas, as well as beliefs in a chiliastic end-state, have collapsed. This state of affairs results in interpretations like Theodor Lessing's *Geschichte als Sinngebung des Sinnlosen (History Seen as Imparting Meaning to the Meaningless* [München, 1921]), or Karl Loewith's *Meaning in History* (Chicago, 1949). Theodor Lessing rightly recognizes that history as "coherence of events" is contingent upon human consciousness. From this, however, he concludes that history is nothing more than a unilateral

Let us consider a typically meaningless story, a "story" which in itself would never make a real story; a trivial incident, of interest only to the reporter, whose job it is to record accidents, and to the persons directly involved in it. A man has an argument with his wife, leaves the house and, blinded by emotion, crosses a street heedless of a rapidly approach-

imposition of individual or collective wish-dreams on unprocessed occurrences. "History," he writes, "originating in desires and volitions, needs and intentions, is a realization of the 'dream-visions' *(Traumdichtungen)* of the human race... meaning of history is solely meaning which I myself give myself, and historical evolution is a development from myself to myself.... Thus any event having historical reality is ultimately nothing more than a mechanical appropriation of the event by human groups for human advantages" *("Ein mechanisches Anereignis vereignet durch Menschengruppen an Hand menschlicher Nutzinteressen," op. cit.,* pp. 10, 15). What Theodor Lessing does not see is the fact that in the process of history subject and object interpenetrate each other, interact with each other, thereby effecting that unique development in which the subject, i.e. human comprehension, gradually becomes an objective fact, namely human consciousness.

To Loewith everything looks simpler. He bases his argument on the popular Western assumption that meaning is equivalent to goal: "It is not by chance," he declares, "that we use the words 'meaning' and 'purpose' interchangeably, for it is mainly purpose which constitutes meaning for us.... History... is meaningful only by indicating some transcendent purpose beyond the actual facts. But since history is a movement in time, the purpose is a goal" *(ibid.,* p. 5). He admits that there may be other kinds of meaning: "This identification of meaning and purpose does not exclude the possibility of other systems of meaning. To the Greeks, for example, historical events and destinies were certainly not simply meaningless—they were full of import and sense, but they were not meaningful in the sense of being directed toward an ultimate end in a transcendent purpose that comprehends the whole course of events" *(ibid.,* p. 6). Loewith does not, however, search for the Greek significance of meaning, and, in speaking of transcendence, he disregards the possibility of an "immanent transcendence": *form.* By thus restricting the sense of meaning, and by seeing history as a mere course of happening, a "movement in time," whereby time is considered to be an abstractly independent dimension, he limits the range of his study, and his question is somehow decided a priori. We have to look closer into the Greek kind of meaning which inheres in their peculiar historical situation and view of the world. And we have to consider the many aspects of time, and the complex interdependence of time and human consciousness. Only then, it seems to me, does the nature of history reveal itself in its full extent.

ing automobile which, swerving to avoid him, jumps the curb and kills a passer-by. This occurrence seems a paradigm of complete meaninglessness. It involves three total strangers connected by mere "accident." They are, to be sure, linked through gapless causality, which makes it perfectly clear that causality does not in itself constitute meaning. It may point toward a meaning, but as such it is purely functional.

This occurrence would become meaningful only if we were to look into its before and after, into the relation of the jaywalker to his wife, the life of the dead man, the irrational guilt feelings, the possibly far-reaching psychic effects in all the survivors. What would to the four people still remain accidental, would, in this way, be raised to a level beyond the persons involved, and we would be made to sense the mysterious nexus of destinies, part of a universal web of destiny in which we, all of us, unknowingly move. Were an author to view the event from this vantage point, he would, by giving it a meaning, or just searching for a meaning, make it into a story.

There is, in fact, an author who has done just this, namely Thornton Wilder in his novel *The Bridge of San Luis Rey*. Part One, entitled "Perhaps an Accident," begins with the report of an incident: "On Friday noon, July the twentieth 1714, the finest bridge in all Peru broke and precipitated five travellers into the gulf below." The fatal accident is witnessed by a monk, brother Juniper, who just a moment before it occurred has stopped at the bridge to wipe his forehead and contemplate with satisfaction the auspicious progress of his missionary work. Thornton Wilder has him ask the big question: Why did this happen to *those* five? And the biographies of these five which brother Juniper searches out reveal that all of them—each in his own way—had simultaneously arrived at the end of their inner lives just prior to the accident. Such tallying is of course extreme; but it shows in the neatest fashion how a mere incident becomes a story—simply through the quest for a meaning. It may well be that we, all of us, are unknowingly enmeshed in a vast and somehow dynamically coordinate coherence, just as a cell is unaware of the organism to which it belongs.

Be that as it may, meaninglessness, non-sense, begins wherever our comprehending faculty fails us, at the ineluctable limits of our capacity; wherever we are blinded and blunder, where our vital power fades. Conversely, wherever we try to seize a segmental coherence, wherever we conceive a meaning, it has vital effects; it exerts a kind of magic, the inherent magic of life itself.

Since a meaningful coherence requires a conscious mind to conceive it, *history can come about and develop only in connection with consciousness*. As man becomes more aware of the coherence of what he does and what happens to him, in like measure he gives it meaning and makes it into history. In this way he creates history, not only theoretically, as a concept, but actually, as reality. For as soon as a concept forms, it starts influencing and changing the actual world. It fuses with actuality, becomes part of it. People gradually come to act in awareness of the new concept. The concept continues effective, and out of conceptually changed reality an ever more elaborate comprehension of coherence, i.e. more and more consciousness, develops which, in turn, further transforms reality. History, then, appears to be an ever widening process of intercreation between conscious comprehension and material reality.

Hence, the vegetable and the animal world have no

22

history, except the one that man, through the broadening scope of his understanding, has given them. The animal has no history because it lacks a conscious memory, an established consciousness of self. In the animal, memory is merely latent, that is to say, it is called up casually, by external stimuli, and their associations; it has never reached a stable, activated continuity, it has not come to form that inner continuum of emotion, thought and action, which constitutes personal identity. Such grasp of inner coherence, of personal identity is a first, rudimentary concept, and without it no concept of any communal and collective identity—the prerequisite of history—is possible.

So history starts in man. But among men: does an average private person have a history? We would not call it that, we call it a career. Even a biography we accord only selected personalities of general significance, "historic" personalities whose lives carry a meaning for their people, or for humanity. Or, when we speak of a "case history" this implies that a certain chain of personal happenings has a bearing on generally, humanly important medical or sociological concerns. History, accordingly, begins in the sphere of the supra-individual, or better, the supraprivate; on the level of groups, of institutions, of peoples. And when we take the term "history" in its integral sense, when we use it without specification, what we have in mind is the history of humanity.

Thus, the more a flow of events becomes meaningful, the more it becomes history. Or, to view the same in the reverse: History develops with the broadening and deepening of the meaning of happenings, i.e. with the expansion of consciousness, of the faculty to conceive coherence, to conceive of communal and collective identity. Meaning, conceived coherence, binds a number of casually, loosely connected happenings into a story. Meaning as a concept of a coherent personal life turns a series of data into a biography. Meaning, be it as purpose or as organic form, articulates a jumble of apparently futile power struggles, endeavors, achievements, and failures, into the specific history of a people, or the history of man. So to deny that history has meaning is to deny that history exists.

In fact, the whole question as to a "meaning of history" has arisen from a recent popular misconception of the term "history." History has come to designate the complex of man's known past while, as we have seen and shall see further, history in its proper sense is by no means restricted to the past, or even characterized by the past. It is no mere complex of settled events, no museum of dead objects. History is a living thing, it is with us and in us every moment of our lives. Not only the informed person, but everybody is in whatever he does constantly moving in history. In his inner life history is archetypally active. In his outer life—political, economic, technological, when he is voting, making a contract, driving a car, watching television—he is continuously manipulating historically rooted concepts and institutions. For his acting and planning he needs the solid foundation of his lifetime's sedimentary memory, that is, his personal identity, but beyond that he would be incapable of leading his daily life in a modern society without the background of a communal memory, without the sense of his national, or human, identity, which is history.

II

THE
HISTORY
OF
HISTORY

1

Our ANALYSIS OF TERMS HAS SHOWN THAT HISTORY presupposes a concept of communal identity, of nationality, or humanity. And this concept of identity makes it *a limine* unimaginable that history is nothing more than a confused, chaotic mass of events, of conflicts, rises, and falls, which human beings have invested with their dreams and illusions. Identity implies continuity, coherence, form.

But, for the sake of confirmation, let us use a different approach. Let us try to understand the phenomenon of history in terms of itself, as a *history of history*. Let us see how history—its concept and actuality—has developed and how it has now come to decay.

The development of the concept of history reflects the development of human consciousness, of man's awareness of himself. An infant starts from the animal level. It lacks an established identity, a coherence of personal existence. Like an animal, it lives in a perpetual present. Hence it has no sense of change. In fact, it refuses to accept change which is utterly disturbing to it and disrupts its world. Children need regularity, a solid, stable foundation of existence, provided by their homes and parents. Of course, they are curious, extremely curious, in their drive to appropriate things, the elements of their world, and gradually to discover relationships. But this appropriation has to take place on the basis of complete normality. Only by tiny steps and variations do they come to learn the *event,* the reality of change. And only through the experience of change do they gain the distance to their own being, which is needed for the formation of the ego.

The childhood of man as a genus displays great similarity to the childhood of the individual. This we can gather from the reports of a great number of nineteenth-century explorers who had a fresher, less dogmatic look at the life of aborigines than present-day anthropologists have—not only because they still encountered native populations who were either untouched or at least much less exposed to influences, exploitations, and questionnaires, but because the explorers themselves were not predirected in their approach by modern sociological and psychological categories. In modern anthropology there occurs a problem analogous to one in physics: The phenomenon observed is changed by the very act of observation.

Certain traits common to aboriginal tribes, infants, and animals suggest that man too in his early stages lived in a changeless world. In the state of "participation"—so admirably described and richly documented by Lucien Lévy-Bruhl[1]—some of these aboriginal tribes feel themselves liv-

---

[1] Lucien Lévy-Bruhl, *Les fonctions mentales dans les sociétés inférieures* (Paris, 1910); *La mentalité primitive* (Paris, 1921); *L'âme primitive,* 3d ed. (Paris, 1927); and, most important: *Les carnets de Lucien Lévy-Bruhl* (Paris, 1949). For comparison with the child cf. Jean Piaget, *La construction du reel chez l'enfant,* Vol. I (Paris, n. d.); Vol. II (Paris, 1937); *La représentation du monde chez l'enfant,* nouvelle édition (Paris, 1947); *Le développement de la notion du temps chez l'enfant* (Paris, 1946).

28

ing on the same level with, and in permanent contact and exchange with the demonized forces of nature, the vegetable and animal tribes. There is little, if any differentiation between waking and dreaming, between species and individual, between past and present, between human and animal existence; and easy transformations, goings and comings, take place across various forms of existence. Change, as constant exchange, is omnipresent and perpetual, it is equivalent to permanence. The present coincides with eternity. Only when the demonic forces are removed and consolidated into deities, can the contrast between change and permanence register.

The probability that such a state of general participation, as has been found prevailing among aboriginal tribes, corresponds to the state of prehistoric man is enhanced by the fact that its traces reach far into the myths, cults, and representations of historical peoples. Myths, even in early historical ages, are not only taken as accounts of reality, they are one with present reality, they continue effective in people's lives. Where myth is alive, people live their myths in perpetual imitation of immemorial patterns. Ancestors are identified with successors, past and present fuse, time is contracted in the permanent moment. Thomas Mann exemplifies such imitative life, such "moving in others' tracks," by his Joseph's teacher Eliezer: "For in him time is cancelled, and all the Eliezers of the past gather to shape the Eliezer of the present, so that he speaks in the first person of that Eliezer who was Abram's servant, though he was far from being the same man."[2]

There is, to be sure, a rudimentary form of communal

[2] *Freud and the Future* (1936) in *Essays of Three Decades* (New York, Inc., 1947), p. 422.

identity in aboriginal tribes. But such feeling of generic identity does not go much beyond the physical cohesion of an animal species. It has not reached a clearly conceptual stage. In aboriginal as well as in mythical life concept and actuality are one.

Among the great cultures of our globe, our Western civilization is the only one to have developed history proper, explicitly and distinctly human history. The Far Eastern cultures could not arrive at this since, until fairly recent times, they have been "arrested"—to use Toynbee's term—at a religious stage, that is to say, in a state where life is suffused with an immovable absolute, which has prevented them from realizing fundamental change.

2

WITHIN WESTERN CIVILIZATION, THE FIRST PEOPLE to whom the phenomenon of change was a crucial, utterly disquieting experience were the *Greeks*. Even their Olympic gods show, by dint of their ceaseless antagonisms, intrigues, terrestrial sorties, a peculiar inconstancy and vulnerability. The pathetic dilemmas deriving from the ambiguous, or even contradictory guidance of the divine powers are reflected in Greek tragedy. Against this dubious stability arose Greek philosophy whose dominant theme might be interpreted as an attempt to reconcile the actuality of change with the none the less indispensable permanence of a cosmic substance and order. The sustained effort toward resolution of this schism led to the development of techniques of logical thought, and ultimately to the perfection of the self-reflecting mind, the generic ego of man. But the Greeks, even in their first awareness of change, could not—paradoxically— strip it of an element of permanence. It remained a delusion of the senses. This is why Greek thinking, diametrically counter to the view of modern positivistic science, did not trust the senses as a last instance. Change was conceived as

31

a wavelike come and go on the surface of stability, a perpetual alternation of ever the same phases, situations, and processes. It retained the character of regularity and perpetuity.

It was *Heraclitus* who for the first time gave striking expression to the experience of change: "You cannot step twice into the same rivers; for fresh waters are ever flowing in upon you."[1] But this sentence reveals only part of his view. It has to be supplemented by other statements: "We step and do not step into the same rivers; we are and are not."[2] Heraclitus actually seems to have seen the cosmos as a *coincidentia oppositorum,* as a fundamental substance diffusing in variety, change, and strife, ever to reunite into the one element it basically is: "it scatters and it gathers; it advances and retires"[3] and "Men do not know how what is at variance agrees with itself. It is an attunement (*harmonía*) of opposite tensions . . ."[4]

These dicta express for the first time a profound, perhaps an ultimate verity, which in a way is as valid today as it was when it was first pronounced. And yet, we have to consider when and where a word is spoken. It makes all the difference whether the same thing is said in the sixth century B.C. or in the twentieth century A.D.; the whole aspect of the statement is changed. In fact, this is precisely what those words of Heraclitus mean. As said by Heraclitus, they show that even this most revolutionary of the pre-Socratic thinkers is unable to conceive of fundamental change—change as a unique process which first had to be experienced before such dicta could gain their full momentum. To Heraclitus

---

[1] Burnet, 4th ed., frs. 41, 42.
[2] *Ibid.,* fr. 81.
[3] *Ibid.,* fr. 40.
[4] *Ibid.,* fr. 45; cf. also frs. 20, 43, 96, 120.

change, movement, strife, although clearly realized, were in themselves steady, as it were, they meant emergence, return, and re-emergence of things from and into the same underlying fiery substance. Movement was still impregnated with substantial immutability.[5]

At the other end of the Hellenic life-span, at the end of the high period of Greece, we find *Aristotle* summing up the whole Greek thinking. He, together with Speusippus, the head of the older academy, is the actual initiator of the idea of evolution, which, in fact, is the very core of his metaphysics. To Plato, all empirical entities, and so also the human being, were still projections of the everlasting realm of absolute Ideas, of which what we call reality was seen to be a mere shadow-replica. Aristotle assumed that the organic being in its development carries its Idea with it, incorporates it, fulfills it in the unfolding of its life. The Idea, to Aristotle, is the very motive power, and at the same time, the aim and end, the forming principle—the *entelechy*—of the developing being. Thus, the Idea, embodied in moving life, is dynamized in Aristotle's concept, and so is life itself. And yet, even so, Aristotle's Idea belongs to an eternal sphere of divinity, it reaches down from this realm of the absolute: the touch of the divine sets life in motion. Aristotle regarded the different levels of organic nature, the vegetable, the animal, and the human, as consecutive evolutionary stages, but evolutionary only in a theoretical, quasi-static sense; that is to say, he took one stage as the essential *premise* of the other, but he did not assume an actual *transformation* of one into the other. The whole, the divine, is prior to the parts, and every organic being is cre-

[5] Cf. Karl Reinhardt, *Parmenides und die Geschichte der Griechischen Philosophie* (Bonn, 1916), pp. 206 f.

ated separately by a new touch of the divine. Accordingly, to Aristotle, humanity has no beginning and no end, but, through recurring catastrophes all civilization is periodically wiped out, and has to be created anew.

So even this elaborate concept of evolution remained suspended in the absolute. It was not an account of one singular happening, it was the principle of an ever recurring process. To be sure, for Aristotle the undifferentiated undulation of Heraclitus' stream of being has extended into articulate, protracted tides, but the career of humanity still appears as a wavelike movement on the surface of eternity.

This could not be otherwise, for the Greeks, at least as long as they were genuinely Hellenic, could not arrive at a lasting notion of humanity as such, and its career, that is history as such. It is true that in the period of the Peloponnesian wars, at the climax and turning point of Greek history, the sophists, through their emphasis on natural as against institutional law (*phýsis* versus *nómos*), were led to the assumption of the basic equality of men, and that the physiological studies ascribed to Hippocrates, probably a disciple of the sophists Prodikos and Gorgias, came to the conclusion that ethnic variants are due to climatic differences. But these views did not take hold of Greek mentality. Hence, the Athenians, the very initiators of democracy, did not think of touching the institution of slavery, and their loftiest minds, Socrates, Plato, Aristotle,[6] and the tragic poets were not concerned about it. The reason for this appears to be that the Greeks did not, until very late, bear the impact of world events, in the broad sense of the word. They had one sworn enemy, the Persians, who had no share

[6] Although born in Stagira, a Greek colony on the Aegean shore, he was educated in Athens.

in their system of values, and who, with the rest of the world, were regarded as a lower order of human beings, as brutes, "barbarians," which originally means, the "stammering," the ones uttering incomprehensible, birdlike, doglike, elemental sounds. Man, in his full measure, free, cultured, reasoning man was still identified with Hellenic man.

So what they directly experienced were but their domestic affairs, which only in the Persian wars and interferences, and in the final Roman conquest were affected by foreign intrusions. These domestic events, however, they experienced with an unprecedented acuity of perception. The encounter with the Persian hordes and despots strengthened their sense of Hellenic, pan-Hellenic identity, and made them conscious of their changing situation. They inaugurated political historiography, intended as factual historiography, in contradistinction to mythography and cosmogony.

Characteristically, the Greek word *historía* meant "physical research." The early Ionian travellers—especially *Hecataeus* (ca. 500 B.C.), the first to focus on the inhabited earth as his special field of study, and, a little later, *Herodotus,* "the father of history"—still combined geography and ethnography with stories of happenings in foreign countries. This original meaning of *historía* points to a mode of historiography which modern scholars are inclined to call scientific, particularly in regard to *Thucydides* (fifth century B.C.), in whose work Greek historiography reached its full maturity. What makes it appear scientific is, apart from its (not always dependable) attempt at factuality, precisely its underlying assumption of a stable, absolute, natural order of things, of a regular and predictable recurrence of events.

Thucydides, too, believed that human processes always repeat themselves; and convinced as he was of the basic stability of human conditions, he sought to derive from history ever valid connections of cause and effect, and general principles of human behavior. But this quasi-scientific Greek view of history, which is also manifest in Aristotle's *Politics,* was by no means the same as that of our modern "historical science" which evolved under the domination of the natural sciences. The Greeks did not yet seek knowledge simply for knowledge's sake, nor essentially for technological and economic advantage. They were not concerned with that aimless amassing of facts, such as is practiced in our historical and social sciences, with that theoretical pragmatism, collecting data for future use, which, even should they be called for, could hardly be reached in the endless files of incoherent material. Greek historical research was pragmatic in a way utterly different from ours: the Greeks wanted to know in order to achieve an orientation in their world, in order to live in the right way; knowledge was closely connected with action, it was indeed part of action. And living and acting in the right way was not necessarily equated with acting *successfully.* It means acting and living in accordance with the cosmic order. Research, empirical as well as speculative, was therefore essentially search for the meaning of the cosmic order, meaning, not as purpose and end—for within eternal recurrence of events no purpose or goal of human life was conceivable—but meaning as established form. From pre-Socratic to Stoic thinking the quest for the meaning of cosmic order, which human conduct had to follow, was the prime motive of inquiry.

History was for Herodotus—as it was for Thucydides—a live and personal experience. The critical clash of the Persian wars appeared to him to manifest a fundamental and everlasting opposition between the Hellenic and the barbarian worlds, and in his work a first glimpse of broader coherence emerged from the form of motley itinerary *(periégēsis)* characteristic of travellers in those days. Thucydides had been a fleet commander in the Peloponnesian wars, and the experience of this inter-Hellenic hegemonial contest— in the compass of his view something like a first world war —moved him to record these events, from which he sought to draw a lesson for conduct in future conflagrations.

The discrepancy between supranatural determination of human life and human attempts at self-assertion becomes increasingly focal to Greek tragic poetry, philosophy, and historiography. The consequence is more paradoxical for the historians than for the tragic poets. Cyclic iteration appears inevitable; indeed it originates in a self-perpetuating guilt of human existence, which has to be continually redeemed through Nemesis.[7] (What most concerns Herodotus in earthly change is the shift in fortune, the rise and fall of the mighty.) But while tragedy shows the futility of human revolt against the will of the gods and the forces of destiny, the historians try to deduce rules of behavior from an apparently ineluctable course of happenings.

The same Greek peculiarities are noticeable in *Polybius,* the third of the Greek pioneers of historiography; only the theme of his historical account is wider in scope and leads him a step farther than his predecessors. He lived at a pivotal moment and witnessed the ultimate crisis of his people, the conquest of Greece by the Romans and the inception of Roman world dominion. He too took part in the event: as statesman and strategist *(hípparchos)* he strove to secure the independence of the Achaean confederation, and to ward off the encroachments of Roman influence. He

[7] Cf. also Pindar's second Olympic ode.

came to Rome as a hostage and was so deeply impressed
by the vigor and efficiency of Roman institutions that he
switched sides while working for the same cause. As friend
and adviser he accompanied Scipio Aemilianus into the
Third Punic War, and after the Roman conquest of Corinth
he served as a mediator between his native Greece and
Rome, preventing destructions and trying to reconcile his
countrymen to the inescapable Roman supremacy. For him,
the fall of Hellas passes over into the glorious ascent of
Rome, on which happenings everywhere seemed to converge. This was the decisive experience of his life: he
planned to set it down in his historical work, and it carried
him beyond all prior conceptions of history. "Previously,"
he writes, "the doings of the world had been, so to say,
dispersed, as they were held together by no unity of initia-
tive, results, or locality; but ever since this date [the 140th
Olympiad, i.e. 220–216 B.C.] history has become an organic whole [*sōmatoeidē,* bodylike], and the affairs of Italy
and Libya have been interlinked with those of Greece and
Asia, all leading up to one end."[8] He also clearly recognized
the Roman reign even in its then early stage as the first true
world dominion: "How striking and grand is the spectacle
presented by the period with which I purpose to deal, will
be most clearly apparent if we . . . compare with the Roman
dominion the most famous empires of the past. . . . The
Persians for a certain period possessed a great rule and
dominion, but so often as they ventured to overstep the
boundaries of Asia they imperilled not only the security
of this empire, but their own existence. . . . The Macedonian
rule in Europe extended but from the Adriatic region to
the Danube, which would appear a quite insignificant por-

[8] Book I, 3, Loeb Classics edition, translation by W. R. Paton.

tion of the continent. Subsequently, by overthrowing the Persian empire they became supreme in Asia also. But though their empire was now regarded as the greatest geographically and politically that had ever existed they left the larger part of the inhabited world as yet outside it. . . . But the Romans have subjected to their rule not portions, but nearly the whole of the world."[9]

The vast confluence and concentration of events which he witnessed resulted in an extended historical concept of whose novelty he himself was proudly aware: "For what gives my work its peculiar quality, and what is most remarkable in the present age is this. Fortune *(tyché)* has guided almost all the affairs of the world in one direction—has forced them to incline toward one and the same end; a historian should likewise bring before his readers under one synoptical view *(hypò mían sýnopsin)* the operations by which she has accomplished her general purpose. Indeed it was this chiefly that invited and encouraged me to undertake my task. . . . As it is, I observe that while several modern writers deal with particular wars and certain matters connected with them, no one, as far as I am aware, has ever attempted to inquire critically when and whence the general and comprehensive scheme of events originated and how it led up to the end. I therefore thought it quite necessary not to leave unnoticed or allow to pass into oblivion this the finest and most beneficent of the performances of Fortune. . . . We can no more hope to perceive this from histories dealing with particular events than to get at once a notion of the form of the whole world, its disposition and order, by visiting, each in turn, the most famous cities, or indeed by looking at separate plans of each. . . . He indeed

[9] *Ibid.,* Book I, 2.

who believes that by studying isolated histories he can acquire a fairly just view of history as a whole, is, as it seems to me, much in the case of one, who, after having looked at the dissevered limbs of an animal once alive and beautiful, fancies he has been as good as an eyewitness of the creature itself in all its action and grace. For could anyone put the creature together on the spot, restoring its form and the comeliness of life [literally: the soul, *tēs psychēs euprepeía*], and then show it to the same man, I think he would quickly avow that he he was formerly very far away from truth and more like one in a dream."[10]

In these epochal sentences, which reveal the powerful impact of his experience, Polybius has hit upon an essential truth which applies today as it did in his time. It is he who first grasps the organic character, the dynamic wholeness of the historical process. He is regarded, and indeed he regarded himself, as the inaugurator of universal, "catholic," history, a *historía koiné, katholiké*. This seems, as seen in retrospect, a little too much to grant him, for his subject is not man as such, not the human world as a supraparticular entity, but still rather the specific community of the Roman world dominion in which he saw the culmination of all previous history. He has, however, reached the broadest concept of historical coherence attainable in his time and place, and the overwhelming experience of Roman expansion stirred in him a first dim notion of the uniqueness of historical happening, although even he could not free himself from the traditional cyclic view.

This, then, was the furthermost limit reached by the Greek, as well as the Roman, idea of history: the notion of the present as an end of all previous happening. The Greeks introduced history—concept and actuality—as a

[10] *Ibid.*, Book I, 4.

coherent development of an ethnic community; but it was history only in a restricted sense, concerning the destiny of a specific people. They did not conceive of *integral* history, that is, history as a single and singular, never recurring flow of happenings, passing through and beyond the individual peoples, history as the career of humanity proper. Change and transformation was seen as a periodical cycle which rhythmically mirrors the rounded order of the cosmos, "a dynamic likeness of eternity . . . a likeness which we have given the name of time."[11] The present appeared as a stage of decadence from a mythical golden age, or, as with Polybius, as a consummation and convergence of previous happenings. Thus, the Greeks have expressed to perfection the *meaning of history as form*. Their view engendered one main trend of historical thought—theories that either follow in the tracks of ancient tradition, or revert to it in reaction against modern developments while at the same time emulating modern science: from Origen, ibn-Khaldun, Machiavelli, Vico, to Nietzsche, Brooks Adams, Spengler, Toynbee, and Sorokin.

But even this first conception of a coherent communal identity was itself part of human history, inasmuch as it was a singular and crucial advance. And this advance proceeded through close interaction of concept and actuality. Experience of and participation in actual events, as we have observed in Herodotus, Thucydides, and Polybius, gave rise to their increasingly articulate concepts of a coherent ethnical identity, and, in turn, these more articulate concepts, merging into actuality, quickened and broadened the course of events. People began to act with a new awareness of their communal identity.

[11] Plato, *Timaeus* 37. Cf. also *Timaeus* 38: "(The moving objects of sensory perception) are but forms of time which imitates eternity in cyclically circular motion."

3

T HE NOTION OF MAN AS SUCH, AS A SUPRA-ETHNIC HIS-
torical entity, and of history as one, unique, coherent course
of human development, originated with the *Jews*. They may
be regarded as the very embodiment of the essentially historical experience. Their record starts with the emigration of
their patriarchal ancestor, and proceeds in an exodus from
captivity; in their early period, they suffered one subjugation
after the other, and were immediately involved in the rises
and falls of the great powers of antiquity, the Assyrian, the
Neo-Babylonian, the Persian, the Hellenistic of Alexander
and the Seleucids, and the Roman. They survived them all
by outlasting their physical, political establishment and
evolving into a spiritually global community, accompany-
ing, or sharing, the destinies of the peoples of the world in
all their ages until this very day. They survived partly
through the transference of their own particular experience
of suffering onto that of historical humanity: they did not
suffer alone; they were compelled to witness and participate
in the suffering of others. Hence they realized change in a
much deeper way than the Greeks—change touched the

core of existence. From the immediate experience of the variety of peoples and epochs, and of the connections between all of them, there emerged the notion of man as one supreme entity, and of the destiny of man as one comprehensive and unique happening.

The world of the Greeks, we have seen, was divided into two coordinate, and yet distinct spheres, the human realm of change, variability, mortal agitation, and the realm of the divine or cosmic permanence—none of them created, but mythically arisen, both of them stable, if only through eternal recurrence. The problem of justifying the all too inconstant human existence was one of adjusting the mortal to the eternal existence.

Jewish life has been unstable from the outset, it was built on quicksand. As Charles Péguy put it: "The most comfortable houses, the best built from stones as big as the temple pillars, the most real of real estate . . . will never mean any more to them than a tent in the desert."[1] They emerged from Bedouin origins, striving to settle down, take root, and expand, the way other peoples did. But this has remained their form of life through the millennia—wandering, emigration and immigration, exile and diaspora, perpetually aimed at an ultimate Land of Promise. It starts with Abraham, the stranger from Ur, it begins to take shape in the Egyptian bondage, and during the grand exodus, and in the Babylonian captivity it reaches its completion and sublimation.

The projection and complement of this kind of existence was their concept of the divine: a God, unbegotten, without mythical genealogy and kinship, without a home place, but

[1] *Notre Jeunesse XI*, 12 (Paris, 1910); translated by Anne and Julien Greene in *Basic Verities* (New York, 1943).

omnipresent, without perceptible shape or name, but with a strongly apprehended impulse and will; indeed pure impulse and will, moving freely like the wind. He is *one* God, supreme, leaving no room for others, having no truck with others, and by all these qualities predestined to integral spirituality, a *spiritus generis* and potential *spiritus generis humani;* a dynamic God, goading and guiding the people, and thereby creating it—hence, in retroprojection, a creator of all things.

The universe is a "creation," made by God and comprehended in him. Man is created; everything has its distinct starting point. Life on earth centers on the human person, such as he is sprung from the divine person's act: Jewish man does not, like Hellenic man, try to approximate the divine order; he is originally fashioned by God in his image and has even grown ever more so, that is, grown *free* through his fall—the stable existential guilt of the mortal, singular being, as it was felt by the Greeks, is dynamized and dramatized by the story of the fall, which unleashes the truly historical destiny of man. For the fall represents a definite *act,* establishing this existential guilt as an exercise of man's free will, and that is, as a *sin,* which man has to atone for, *can* atone for through action, indeed through consistent striving throughout his whole life and throughout the Jewish generations. The Greek cosmos is impersonal, and man is constitutionally, irrevocably guilty. He can try to live in accordance with this cosmic order—hence his search for the nature of this order. But in exercising his will, he gets more and more enmeshed in the thicket of fate. His guilt, inseparable from his mortality, and hence self-perpetuating, is inevitably followed by Nemesis. No instance exists to whom he is unequivocably responsible, nobody whom he can make responsible for his predicament; nothing but his own mortal nature whose incongruence with the cosmic order causes all adversity. There are no commandments to be obeyed, the nature of the cosmos must be understood and followed.

For the Jews, the order of the world and of man's life has been established by God once and for all and, while the creator himself must be kept beyond all doubt and blemish, his creation is perpetually in question. There exists a Lord of all things who can be argued with, who is made responsible for the responsibility with which he has saddled the human being. Since the defectiveness of the creation and the defection of man bears upon the integrity of the creator, man, in order to save this image of perfection has to take upon himself, upon his sinful free will, all failure and suffering he has to undergo. Hence the dialectical relationship of Jewish man to his God with whom he has a covenant, with whom he wrangles, but whom he ultimately justifies with his own guilt. Man's guilt is implied in his freedom, it has established his freedom. The Greek existential guilt is turned into wilfully enacted guilt—the cosmic problem has become a moral problem. Consequently, man has a concrete task of atonement: just as he has wilfully sinned, he has wilfully to rectify the faultiness of his ways, he has to strive, freely and intentionally, to restore the order intended by God, which he, man, has intentionally transgressed: he has to do his part to realize the Kingdom of God on Earth, which is the actual Promised Land. But such ordained achievement is no mere restoration, as was the Greek eternal recurrence; *man's striving makes it into a new and unique happening*. A goal is set for humanity; a future, *the* future is created as the deciding factor in man's destiny. History assumes *meaning as purpose*. The uniqueness of the process, the integration of the past, not only into the present, but into a future, initiates true history.

But aside from this temporal integration, the development of Judaism demonstrates on an enlarged scale that other property of true history: the interaction of concept and actuality. The exodus from Egypt, the experience of migration, homelessness, and life in a state of promise, the subordination to an aim and discipline of an aim—hence the tables of the law—have created integral Jewish monotheism, the concept of, not just one, but *the* one, omnipresent God, of God, the leader, the commander, the creator; and the Biblical record of the migration shows how this concept, in turn, created the people and its sense of tribal identity. The experience of successive captivities and subjections gradually sublimated and spiritualized the concept, and resulted in a clear awareness of the identity of humanity proper which the Jews felt chosen—blessed and condemned —to keep alive at their own peril.

The awareness of the identity of man is closely connected with, indeed implied in, the notion of the "chosen people." More explicitly than the story of creation, the account of the tower of Babel (Gen. *11*:1–8) makes it clear that God is originally the God of all men: "Behold, the people is *one,* and they have all one language . . . and now nothing will be restrained from them, which they have imagined to do." The arrogant project of the tower "whose top may reach unto heaven" is an exalted reassertion of human freedom, a second fall, as it were, and God's "confound[ing] their language" and "scatter[ing] them abroad . . . upon the face of the earth" is equivalent to a second expulsion. This explicit creation of the *diversity* of mankind confirms its original *unity.* And so does God's complementary move, his covenant with Abraham and later with Jacob—who becomes, and engenders, Israel—and God's preference of him over the first-born Esau, which gave rise to the notion of the "chosen people" (and, as will be seen later, to the Christian concept of predestination). This preference of Israel is contingent upon a mission, a training as it were for the salvation of the heathen, it is from Abraham on, down through all Biblical generations, a blessing tainted with the prediction of suffering and desolation.[2] Both, the dispersion of mankind and the mission of the "chosen people" signify the inclusion of all peoples of the world in one and the same system of values, in contrast with the Greeks' feeling basically alien to the barbarians. There is ample further evidence of this early realization of human identity: so the commands of brotherly love for the stranger, explicitly referring to the Jews' past experience of being "strangers in the land of Egypt" (Lev. 19:34); or the Lord's admonition through Amos (about 760 B.C.): "Are ye not as children of the Ethiopians unto me, O children of Israel? . . . Have not I brought up Israel out of the land of Egypt? and the Philistines from Caphtor, and the Syrians from Kir?"[3]

---

[2] Gen. 15:13; Deut. 28:25, 28–29, 34, 37, 43–44, 64–66; 29:24–26, and so forth, down to Isa. 49–54.
[3] Amos 9:7.

4

OUT OF JUDAISM, INDEED WITHIN JUDAISM, EVOLVED *Christianity*. It evolved with the Jewish concept of human identity. Step by step, propelled by woeful experiences, the Jewish aim kept broadening, from tribal liberation to human salvation: the Promised Land shifted from parochial Canaan to the Kingdom of God on Earth; the God-anointed political leader (*Mashiach,* Messiah) became the ultimate judge and prince of peace[1] and the "servant of God"; the distinction between punishment and reward dwindled, suffering became excellence, abasement was elevation.[2] The God of Vengeance and Retribution[3] was sublimated into the God of Justice,[4] and finally into the God of Mercy and Peace.[5] In this process the three history-generating Jewish tendencies converge: *missionarism, messianism, eschatology.*[6]

[1] Isa. *11*:1–9.
[2] Isa. *42*:1–7; *49*:3, 6–10; *50*:4–6; *53*:3–5, 7–11; *55*:5.
[3] Exod. *20*:5, 21, 23–26; Deut. *19*:21.
[4] Ezek. *18*.
[5] Hos. *2*:15, 18–19; *6*:6; *11*:8–9; Mic. *6*:8; Jonah *4*:2, 10–11.
[6] This evolution, as indeed all evolution, is not a chronologically rectilinear one; it is, up to the late prophets and Jesus, one of varying, but growing prevalence. We have also to take into account that the Old Testament is a compound of intermingled writings from different periods.

48

Two developments were decisive in the catholization of the historical trend: the turn from *messianism* to *Christology* and the gradual *elucidation of the road to salvation*.

The captivity and migration of the Jews had transformed the expectation, frequent among ancient Oriental peoples, of a benevolent ruler who would restore order and well-being, like the Egyptian "shepherd king," into the notion of an anointed leader to the Promised Land; and subsequent tribulations had made this Messiah into an ultimate deliverer and judge of the hard-pressed people. From the rule of the Seleucids in the second century B.C. the eschatological tension grew under mounting calamities into a true paroxysm: the Kingdom of God was believed quite near.

As early as in "Deutero-Isaiah" (eighth century B.C.) and the so-called "Trito-Isaiah" (about 450 B.C.) the Day of Salvation had been envisioned as the creation of a "new heaven" and "a new earth": "the heavens shall vanish away like smoke, and the earth shall wax old like a garment, and they that dwell therein shall die in like manner: but my salvation shall be for ever, and my righteousness shall not be abolished . . . fear ye not the reproach of men, neither be ye afraid of their revilings[7] . . . the redeemed of the Lord shall return, and come with singing unto Zion . . . they shall obtain gladness and joy; and sorrow and mourning shall flee away . . . Behold, I have taken out of thine hand the cup of trembling . . . thou shalt no more drink it again, but I will put it into the hand of them that afflict thee; which have said to thy soul, Bow down, that we may go over: and thou hast laid thy body as the ground, and as the street, to them that went over."[8]

In the apocalyptic conditions under the rule of the Idu-

[7] Isa. *51*:6–7.
[8] Isa. *51*:11, 22–23.

49

maean Herods and the Roman procurators, the advent of the Kingdom of God appearing imminent, Jesus brought the traditional prophecy to its climax: he no longer merely heralded the Last Judgment, but he himself assumed the role of the long-awaited Messiah. This is as far as a Jewish community, even in its extreme vanguard, that is, Jesus himself and his original disciples, could go. (Pretenders to the role of Messiah emerged later again under stress[9]). Even the promise of resurrection of the righteous had long been current among the prophets and in the apocalypses. But the deification of Jesus, which meant the humanization of God, was unacceptable to the Jews; it would have shattered their concept of God.

Nevertheless, this radically new beginning—the Hellenistic Paul's breaking of the old Covenant, the belief in Jesus' filial incarnation of God and in his Second Coming, as already substantiated by an effected resurrection, i.e. the past guaranteeing the future—enhanced the emphasis on the future and made the historical process more concrete.

The second development that strengthened historical awareness was the increasing elaboration of the stages and periods of man's road to salvation. The Greek view of human happenings establishing *meaning as form,* constituted, as we have seen, a dynamization of eternity through the assumption of a cyclic recurrence of events. The Jewish and Christian notion of man's road to salvation created *meaning as purpose* and initiated the uniqueness of change, that is, the actual history of man. But in a peculiar way the cyclic

[9] David Alroy in the eleventh, Reubeni in the sixteenth, Sabbatai Zewi in the seventeenth, and Jacob Frank in the eighteenth century.

view contributed to the further elaboration of the new vision: in Hellenistic Judaism the theory of cycles appears incorporated into the message of salvation through a periodization of its progression.

The cyclic periodicity springs from two sources, a cosmic and a mythically human one, both probably of ancient Oriental origin. The first reaches its final form in the Stoic representation of a "cosmic year," or "big year," constituting a periodical recurrence of the same astronomical constellation *(apokatástasis)* and corresponding re-creation *(palingenesía)* and repetition of every single event. This cosmic year, following the revolution *(períodos)* of the planets, is, by analogy with the vernal and autumnal equinox, divided into two seasons, winter and summer, each climaxing in an earthly catastrophe, a hibernal *flood (kataklysmós)* and an aestival *conflagration (ekpýrōsis)*. From each of these catastrophes the world with all its happenings rises anew. This Stoic theory of aeons, as anticipated by Aristotle (according to Censorinus) and a reference in Plato's *Timaeus*,[10] and even earlier by Heraclitus[11] and the Pythagoreans, goes back, in all probability, to the Babylonian priests who were among the earliest to observe and compute the periodicity of celestial movements, and to connect them astrologically with human events. The cyclic periodicity of world happenings, and the whole theory of eternal recurrence, seem to have issued from those Babylonian observations.[12] The inclusion of the two equinoctial seasons made the original bipartition into our common four seasons.

[10] *Timaeus* 22d.
[11] Cf. Karl Reinhardt, *Parmenides und die Geschichte der Griechischen Philosophie* (Bonn, 1916), pp. 206 f.
[12] Cf. Bernhard Sticker, *Weltzeitalter und astronomische Perioden,* Saeculum IV/3, pp. 241–249.

The other ancient periodization that has come down to us in Hesiod's *Works and Days* (eighth century B.C.) and in the Zoroastrian *Avestas* appears like an application of celestial periods to human stages. The four human ages of Hesiod are, as is well-known, represented by successive generations which are characterized by metals. His mythical anthropogeny continues his theogony in a descending line, from a golden, paradisiac, to a silver, and a brazen age down to the iron age in which the poet lived, and which, through internecine war and general corruption, has sunk into irretrievable misery.

This anthropogeny seems to reflect an experience common among primeval peoples: the lapse from a mythical state of harmony of the tribe, indeed of life, into one of discord, rupture of peace, i.e. incipient individuation. Hesiod's myth of man's descent from a golden age of gentle mortality, "like going to sleep," an age "far from toil and hardships," to an age of violence and distress, corresponds to the Biblical myth of man's expulsion from paradise into mortality and drudgery. For the Greeks this notion of decadence was somewhat allayed by the belief in cyclic recurrence. The Jews, whose earthly career actually started from misery, introduced, with their prophecies, a shift of emphasis from descent to ascent. Traces of the cyclic view still persisted in the expectation of a return to the original paradisiac state,[13] but the long stretch of successive visitations made this return into a unique occurrence, all the more singular since it was to be brought about with the help of the conscious efforts of the righteous among the people.

[13] Mic. *4*:3–4; Ezek. *34*:25–31; Hos. *2*:18; Isa. *2*:4; *11*:6–8. Such identification of the end-state with the original Eden continues in the late Jewish apocalypses.

In the Jewish-Hellenistic book of Daniel (second century B.C.), the earliest extant apocalypse, the cyclic view is made instrumental to the message of the advent of the Savior by means of the periodization of decadence. The four mythical ages are metaphorically identified with the four historical powers which had successively subjugated the Jews. The book gives us two variants of this combination, one in the second chapter, and another in the seventh and eighth chapters; the first written probably before, the second during, or after the reign of the Seleucid Antiochus Epiphanes.[14] Both of them are prophecies a posteriori and merge into the eschatology of the time.

The second chapter relates a dream of the Babylonian King Nebuchadnezzar and its interpretation by Daniel. The king had seen an image, "[His] head was of fine gold, his breast and his arms of silver, his belly and his thighs of brass. His legs of iron, his feet part of iron and part of clay." And "a stone was cut out without hands, which smote the image upon his feet that were of iron and clay, and brake them to pieces. Then was the iron, the clay, the brass, the silver, and the gold, broken to pieces together . . . and the wind carried them away, that no place was found for them: and the stone that smote the image became a great mountain, and filled the whole earth."[15]

In Daniel's interpretation, the declining ages of man were viewed as the synchronous picture of four great kingdoms degenerating from the golden head, which was the Babylonian king, to the last kingdom—evidently the divided

[14] Cf. H. Louis Ginsberg, *Studies in Daniel,* Texts and Studies of the Jewish Theological Seminary in America, Vol. XIV (New York, 1948); on apocalypses in general: F. C. Burkitt, *Jewish and Christian Apocalypses* (London, 1914).

[15] Dan. 2:32–35.

Hellenistic one—whose iron footing was mixed with clay "so the kingdom shall be partly strong, and partly broken. . . . And in the days of these kings shall the God of heaven set up a kingdom, which shall never be destroyed: and . . . shall break in pieces and consume all these kingdoms, and it shall stand for ever."[16] This seems to indicate that with the downfall of the fourth kingdom the whole edifice of pagan tradition would crumble when the Kingdom of God would appear.

The seventh and eighth chapters of the book describe a dream of Daniel himself showing him the sequence of the four kingdoms in the shape of "four great beasts" rising out of the sea, "diverse one from another." The last two kingdoms are pictured as a ram with two horns, explicitly identified as the kings of Media and Persia, and a he goat with one big horn, which "smote the ram, and brake his two horns," representing "the king of Grecia," i.e. Alexander. And "the he goat waxed very great: and when he was strong, the great horn was broken; and for it came up four notable ones toward the four winds of heaven"—the kingdoms of the Hellenistic diadochi. "And out of one of them came forth a little horn, which waxed exceedingly great . . . even to the host of heaven . . . even to the prince of the host, and by him the daily sacrifice was taken away, and the place of his sanctuary was cast down. . . . And . . . when the transgressors are come to the full, a king of fierce countenance . . . shall stand up . . . against the Prince of princes; but he shall be broken without hand."[17] This "king of fierce countenance" is evidently Antiochus Epiphanes.

In these visions, then, we see the Greek mythical theory

[16] Dan. 2:42–44.
[17] Dan. 8:5–11, 20–21, 23–25.

of the four declining ages of man adapted to the concrete historical experience of the Jewish people, and linked to the eschatological ascent. In addition, there existed at that time in the Near East a traditional pattern of historical periodization, which the Book of Daniel may have blended with the Greek mythical theory. In Achaemenian Persia a record of three great monarchies—the Assyrian, the Median, and the Persian—had been used for the glorification of the conquering dynasty.[18] The Jews did not recall successive conquests, only consecutive subjections and oppressions. So the Book of Daniel starts from the Neo-Babylonian (Chaldaean) Kingdom, which had put an end to the Kingdom of Judaea and destroyed Jerusalem—the predominant memory of this destruction and of the Babylonian captivity seems to have overshadowed the reminiscence of the previous Assyrian subjugation of Israel. But the chronologically unwarranted insertion of the Medians in the eschatological visions is probably due to the influence of the Persian tradition which must have been widespread at the time.

After the disintegration of the fourth, Graeco-Macedonian Kingdom of Alexander, a fifth kingdom was expected to come and was envisioned differently by different peoples. The tribes of the Seleucid Kingdom, resenting the Greek supremacy, hoped for the emergence of an independent native regime. Roman authors, after the defeat of the Syrian Antiochus III by Scipio (Asiaticus) in the battle of Magnesia (190 B.C.), began to extol the rise of an everlasting Roman world dominion. Only the Jews expected the Kingdom of God.

[18] Cf. Ginsberg, loc. cit.; and Joseph Wand Swain, *"The Theory of the Four Monarchies,"* Classical Philology (Chicago), Vol. XXXV, No. 1 (January, 1940), pp. 1–21.

5

JUDAISM HAS REMAINED SUSPENDED IN A STATE OF EX-
pectation, a state of perpetually momentary expectation of
the ultimate event. This could not be otherwise, because
they were never able to conceive its palpable realization, in-
sisting as they did on the absolute purity of the Lord and of
his Kingdom. The imperfectness of human nature had impressed itself so deeply upon their minds that they did not
dare to imagine human beings capable of satisfying the demands of integral righteousness—even their most saintly
men, Moses, Aaron, the prophets, and so Jesus, they could
not bring themselves to see flawless. Therefore, the advent
of the Messiah, must, of necessity, be delayed indefinitely.
It is one of the paradoxes of Judaism that precisely this people which steadfastly insisted that the Kingdom of God
materialize here on earth, contravened any divine incarnation by its extreme sublimation of God.

While Jewish missionarism, messianism, and eschatology
created history as a unique and generally human process,
the Christian establishment of Jesus, not only as "Christ,"
the "anointed," but as the divine redeemer of all mankind,
crystallized it in an event, which was indeed *the* event par

excellence. The chosen people—represented by the "servant of God" whom the Lord had given "for a light to the Gentiles," but "whom man despiseth . . . whom the nation abhorreth," who gave [his] back to the smiters" and "hid not [his] face from shame and spitting"[1] was the antecedent and prefiguration of the personified savior who concentrated in his instantaneously manifest sacrifice the extended victimization of Israel. The Passion of the Jews was a *process,* the Passion of Jesus was an *event.*

Indeed, disregarding its religious and revelatory significance, and viewing it simply as a historical phenomenon, we can scarcely avoid recognizing it as an *epochal event,* an event set in its crucially appropriate moment, its true *kairós,* prepared as it was not only by the climax of an age-old Jewish expectation, but by all the manifold converging trends of the time, spiritual and actual: the Hellenistic mingling of peoples and ideas fanned the already frenzied popular imagination and augmented the Jewish eschatological tradition with all kinds of mythological and speculative material. The syncretistic mysteries, dynamic celebrations of death and resurrection of chthonic deities, began everywhere to prevail over the old static rites. The deification of Roman emperors—sheer individuals without mythical, or even indigenous descent—shrank the distance between the divine and the terrestrial spheres. The universal-minded Stoic philosophy, itself a result of Hellenistic commingling, created a general climate favoring attitudes and values close to those of original Christianity: composure and imperturbability *(ataraxía),* pneumatic concept of the deity,[2] enhanced guilt feeling, cosmopolitism and human equality, love of the

---

[1] Isa. *49*:6–7, *50*:6.
[2] The whole multiform world was seen to have issued from, and to return into the *pneuma* (vital breath and creative spirit) of the deity in circular recurrence, in fact, to *be* this divine systole and diastole.

fellowman, indeed giving aid even to enemies *(opem ferre etiam inimicis)*.[3] To the Stoic Chrysippus fate and predicament coincides with divine providence: *heimarménē* turns into *prónoia*. Finally, the accomplished Roman world empire has furnished the consolidated territorial expanse necessary for Christianity to spread its message effectively. The Latin poet Prudentius (fourth century A.D.) went as far as to proclaim that God had directed the Romans to conquer the world in order to pave the way for Christian world religion.[4]

None of these originally independent agents could have produced by itself the crucial turn toward the uniqueness and ascent of human history, conceptual as well as actual, extending and ramifying through two millennia. The founding Jewish tradition, including Jesus himself, could not have penetrated very far beyond the vigorously guarded fence of its law. The deification of the Roman emperors had been a repeated, but isolated occurrence without any deep and lasting purport for human existence. Nor did the death and resurrection of deities in the Hellenistic mysteries originally carry any implication of commitment for their human participants, who were connected with them only in a sense similar to primeval "participation." Another Latin writer and Christian convert, Minucius Felix (third century A.D.), derided the recurrent futility of these celebrations: "They do not cease to lose every year what they have found, and to find what they have lost. Is it not ridiculous to worship what you mourn and to mourn what you worship?"[5]

It is only the simultaneous convergence and interaction

[3] Seneca, *De Otio*, 1:4.
[4] *Contra Symmachum.*
[5] *Octavius.*

of these agents, and their transformatory fusion by Paul, that has made the action and passion of Jesus into a unique, decisive event and a turning point of human history.[6] The confluence of conditioning agents producing the decisive event, a phenomenon of exemplary importance for the understanding of the working and meaning of history, has not been sufficiently considered in its strictly historical significance because the theological concern habitually interferes. In the blindness to this historical phenomenon, strangely enough, the Roman pagan and the modern protestant theologian concur. "Jews and Christians," Celsus, a Latin Platonist of the second century A.D. writes, "appear to me like a crowd of bats or ants emerging from their haunts, or like frogs sitting by a pool, or worms gathering in a corner of a dunghill, and saying to each other: To us God reveals everything. He does not care about the rest of the world. We are the only ones with whom he converses. . . . Since some among us happened to have sinned, God himself will come or will send his son, to burn these sinners and let us partake of eternal life."[7] It is natural enough that an unconverted Roman in the second century A.D. treats an annoying subversive movement as a ludicrous parochial affair. But the modern theologian Oscar Cullmann who describes the epochal significance of Christianism for the conception

---

[6] Islam, deriving from the Judaeo-Christian tradition, and adapting it to Arabic tribal forms, radiated mostly into the Orient where it competed with the much more ancient Hindu and Sino-Japanese civilizations. Mohammed's *Jihad*, or Holy War, which started the Islamic expansionist movement, was at first an equivalent to the Jewish fight against pagan residues, and evolved later into a challenging countermovement to Christian missionary expansion. Islam has not advanced lastingly beyond its Oriental and African orbit, nor has it produced a civilization surpassing that of the West. We witness on the contrary, the Islamic, along with all other cultures of the world, becoming more and more Westernized, inevitably, and in many respects, deplorably.

[7] Origen, *Contra Celsum*, IV, 23.

of historical time with extraordinary clarity actually confirms Celsus' view by attributing the crucial turn exclusively to the Christian revelation: "the stress on the history of a small people," he declares, "the combining of its external history with facts that, historically regarded, are at best to be called *'faits divers'* (sundry odd facts) . . . and especially the explanation of the whole from that mid-point, the work of Jesus of Nazareth, which taken by itself only belongs to the *'faits divers'* of the history of the Roman empire—all these things must make history appear to the 'pure historian' as a completely arbitrary compilation, which he will reject as being no valid norm to use in passing judgment on the entire sweep of history . . . it takes on meaning only when this central historical action of Jesus of Nazareth is recognized as *absolute divine revelation* to men. Without this faith . . . that history must actually seem to be without meaning."[8]

In point of fact, however, considering the totality of developments before and after the rise of Christianity *on purely historical grounds,* we are, I think, justified to recognize this event as a turning point fixing in earthly time the Jewish creation of the concept and actuality of the uniqueness of human happening, that is, of history. The developments of Jewish messianism and eschatology, of the dynamization and this-worldliness of cults, of the Hellenistic Stoa, and of the Roman Empire, are genuine historical processes which converged in the Christian event, and we need no revelation to see in this event a comprehensive result and at the same time a beginning. In it past, present, and future are sharply distinguished, and yet vitally connected. The new faith produced a first clear *awareness of*

[8] Oscar Cullmann, *Christ and Time* (Philadelphia, 1950), pp. 22 f.

the new, of total newness which is the essence of uniqueness. A new world has emerged, not a renewal of the same, as in the recurrent aeons. A "new creature"[9] was proclaimed to have arisen, and the human being appeared changed, and therefore changeable. The church fathers were the first violently to reject the cyclic view.

The new chronology initiated by the Roman abbot Dionysius Exiguus in 525 A.D. which took as a starting point a non-mythical and approximately ascertainable event, namely the birth of Jesus Christ, is but an expression of this basic turn. To be sure, this datum became a "temporal midpoint"[10] only when, in the eighteenth century, the custom was established to reckon not only forward, but also backward from the birth of Christ. But it is important to note that this system of chronology has outlasted all previous and following reckonings, from the Seleucid and Diocletian to the Fascist, and is becoming, in the present, thoroughly secular era, gradually accepted all over the globe.

[9] II Cor. 5:17.
[10] Cullman, *op. cit.*, p. 18.

6

U P TO THIS POINT WE HAVE CONTEMPLATED THE CON-
ditioning antecedents and the genesis of history, a gradual
process in which it is hardly possible to separate the conceptual from the actual stages; they proceeded by what I would
call a chain interaction.

We shall now follow up the consequences of the establishment of man's historical existence: the process of *secularization* which involves an increasing *dynamization* of the
existence of man and his world.

In all periods preceding the Christian event, and most
particularly in the Christian era, the innermost concern of
man was his relation to a sphere of permanence, a sphere
beyond human mutability and sensory deception. And yet,
*in the Christian event itself the foundation was laid for the
full emancipation of the secular sphere, which means, for
consummate historization.*

Original Christianity still viewed the career of man in
accordance with Jewish eschatological tradition, that is, as
a movement of life, to be sanctified and fulfilled *here below,*
in a Kingdom of God in which heaven and earth become

one. The disciples of Jesus had grown up on Jewish tradition and in the climate of the apocalypses; they expected a Second Coming of Christ in the very near future. Even the early Christian writers believed the Roman Empire to be the fourth and final monarchy before the advent of the terrifying Last Judgment, and in their extreme apprehensiveness they even prayed for the preservation of Rome.[1]

For the faithful in this critical period, therefore, the ascent to the Kingdom of God proceeded *in time,* a unilevel, terrestrial time; there was no deviation into a transcendent beyond. Eternity was no second, superior sphere of timeless existençe, it was just "infinite time." Under the constant stress of overwhelming experiences, Christians moved naively in the stream of events and were as yet unaware of certain momentous discrepancies latent in the teachings of *Paul.* The man who later was forced to grapple with these incompatibilities and to draw the inevitable conclusions was Augustine.

In the *Epistle to the Romans,* Paul says: "Know ye not, that so many of us as were baptized into Jesus Christ were baptized into his death? . . . if we have been planted together in the likeness of his death, we shall be also in the likeness of his resurrection: knowing this, that our old man is crucified with him, that the body of sin might be destroyed, that henceforth we should not serve sin. For he that is dead is freed from sin. Now if we be dead with Christ, we believe that we shall also live with him . . ."[2] And in the *Epistle to the Colossians* it is said: "If ye then be risen with Christ, seek those things which are above, where Christ

[1] Cf. H. H. Rowley, *Darius the Mede and the Four World Empires in the Book of Daniel* (Cardiff, 1935), pp. 73 ff.
[2] Rom. 6:3–8.

sitteth on the right hand of God. Set your affection on things above, not on things on the earth. For ye are dead, and your life is hid with Christ in God. . . . Mortify therefore your members which are upon the earth . . ."[3]

Here is the onset of that crucial division of the physical and the spiritual spheres which subsequently kept growing to the point of complete secularization of human life on earth, and so of history. In the Jewish pilgrimage to the Kingdom of God, however infinitely protracted, life on earth was not separated from life in the spirit. Within earthly life and time man, every man, was called on to contribute toward the ultimate realization of the divinized world. The deification of Jesus Christ, however, and the assumption of the vicarious passion by which he absolves all true believers —as dogmatically interpreted by Paul—generated an inescapable contradiction. On the one hand, the advent of the Kingdom of God on earth, preceded by the Day of Judgment, was still expected to occur in the near future with the *parousia* of Jesus Christ. On the other hand, the baptism of the individual believer, his having died and risen again with Christ and thereafter "living in Christ," forestalled and anticipated for that individual the effect of the Second Coming; and this anticipation implied a deadening to earthly life, and aiming at "things which are above, and not [at] things on the earth," a "life . . . hid with Christ in God," and mortification of the "members which are upon the earth." Thus, a life in this world, a life in time, where the Kingdom of God has yet to come, severs with a hidden life "above," where the salvation of the individual believer is already achieved. The unique descent of God into human form guaranteed earthly realization of salvation, and this

[3] Col. 3:1–3, 5.

"event par excellence" consolidated history on earth. But the unsustainable tension between the above and the below, which Paul derived from it, gave rise to a development which was bound ultimately to surrender history to complete secularity.

This development was greatly furthered by two main consequences of Pauline doctrine: *the changed significance of sin,* and *the new relationship of Christian man to the earthly community.*

For Judaism, man was, by reason of his fall, i.e. of his becoming actually human, a constitutionally fallible creature. But, in principle, he was not necessarily sinful. By his original fall he was endowed with the ability to distinguish good and evil and with the faculty to choose between them. He was no longer constitutionally innocent, since he had acquired knowledge. But the choice between righteousness and sin was left to his free will. Hence God's constant quarrel with man, his perpetual goading him toward the good, and his punishing of the bad. Hence also God's demand on man to contribute by his acts and behavior, by the whole conduct of his life, to the realization of the Kingdom of God. Even Jesus, in the Sermon on the Mount, urged men to "be . . . perfect, even as your Father which is in heaven is perfect."[4]

In the time of the apocalypses, when the great turning was believed close at hand, the feeling of sinfulness rose to extreme intensity and became a powerful agent in the Christian event. In the *First Epistle of John,* a post-Pauline document of uncertain authorship from the second century A.D., we read: *"Herein is love, not that we loved God, but that he loved us, and sent his Son to be the propitiation for*

[4] Matt. 5:48.

our sins."[5] This sentence tells the fundamental reversal of the relationship of man and God. Man is purified not by his own active conduct, but by the undeserved receipt of God's *grace*. Man's justification is not the cause, but the result of divine salvation, for what releases him from his sinful state is solely his *faith* in the divine sacrifice, and baptism, which confirms his faith. This implies that before baptism human beings are inescapably sinful because otherwise God's sacrifice would be meaningless for the righteous, and faith and baptism would have nothing to absolve them from. Thus, the *Christological reversal of man's relation to God* led inevitably to the *doctrine of original sin,* to *man's justification by grace and faith,* and ultimately to the *doctrine of predestination.* The doctrine of predestination, a direct conclusion from the belief in man's justification by grace, traces back to the Jewish notion of the "chosen people." Paul, in *Romans,* chapter 9, explicitly refers to God's election of Jacob and rejection of Esau: "They are not all Israel, which are of Israel: neither, because they are the seed of Abraham, are they all children: but, in Isaac shall thy seed be called. That is, They which are the children of the flesh, these are not the children of God: but the children of the promise are counted for the seed. . . . As it is written, Jacob have I loved, but Esau have I hated. . . . For he saith to Moses, I will have mercy on whom I will have mercy, and I will have compassion on whom I will have compassion. So then it is not of him that willeth, nor of him that runneth, but of God that sheweth mercy. . . . Therefore hath he mercy on whom he will have mercy, and whom he will he hardeneth."[6] "And if by grace, then is it no more of works: otherwise grace is no more grace."[7]

[5] I John 4:10.
[6] *Rom.* 9:6–8, 11, 13, 15–16, 18.
[7] *Rom.* 11:6.

Viewing this process from the Jewish origins, we recognize the whole consistency and import of the shift of emphasis in the relationship of man to God: Jesus Christ's vicarious redemption means the dispensation of the human being from the duty to work for the Kingdom of God on Earth. From this there follows justification by faith alone, and the doctrine of original sin with the promise of salvation through grace alone—an arbitrary, selective grace—and repudiation of life in the flesh. This inevitably leads to the secularization of human life.

Even more influential in this direction is a second consequence of the Christian doctrine: the relation of the faithful to the earthly community. Since Paul, the community of Christ has been a purely universal community in which all are "children of God by faith in Christ Jesus. . . . There is neither Jew nor Greek, there is neither bond nor free, there is neither male nor female: for ye are all one in Christ Jesus. And if ye be Christ's, then are ye Abraham's seed, and heirs according to the promise."[8] Already in the Old Testament the claim to universality had been raised, and being a "light to the Gentiles" had been the Jewish mission. But here for the first time, by Paul, all of man's earthly roots are cut. The believer in Christo is, as such, divested of all earthly origin and condition. Insofar as he lives in Christ, his "Kingdom is not of this world," and "[his] conversation is in heaven."[9] To be sure, he is still involved in earthly circumstances, being a Greek or a Roman, a free man or a slave, and a citizen of the empire. But this is a transitory state. What happens in this interim is of little importance and the submission to the

[8] *Gal. 3*:26, 28–29.
[9] *Phil. 3*:20.

worldly authority, the "rendering unto Caesar the things which are Caesar's" is a compromise of indifference. We should never forget that it was prescribed as a means to consuming a short interval until the day of deliverance, not as a stable condition, as instituted by Luther. This is evidenced not only by the continuing computations of the actual date of Christ's advent, but by the complete disinterest in Roman affairs, which the Christians exhibited. The *Epistle to Diognetus,* an apologetic document of the second century A.D., describes their status and behavior: "They live, each of them, in their native countries, but as strangers *(pároikoi).* They . . . endure everything, in the way of aliens *(xénoi).* Any foreign country is their fatherland, and any fatherland a foreign land . . . They live in the flesh, but not according to the flesh. They spend their life on earth, but they are citizens of heaven."[10] But why then, the Romans expostulated with them, did they still multiply on earth, engender and educate children, partake of the fruits of the earth, and occupy themselves with matters of life? Why did they not all go together into the desert?[11]

To do this would have conflicted with the Christian mission, which, in order to save human souls "for the sake of the eternal life", called for the Christianization of the empire. When this was accomplished under Constantine, it was seen as a providential confirmation of the divine message. The belief of the Romans in the sempiternity and indestructibility of their empire—the everlasting fifth world empire—had, in a modified form, taken hold of the Christian apologists: For them, Rome was the final monarchy before

[10] *A Diognète,* édition critique, trad. et comm. de Henri Marrou (Paris, 1951), pp. 62 ff.
[11] Celsus, quoted by Origen, *Contra Celsum,* VIII, 55.

the advent of the divine whose possible date was fearfully discussed. Hence the Christianization of the empire could be interpreted as a transitional step toward the Kingdom to come. Christians still hoped to settle down for a while in this preparatory stage. Theologians, among them Augustine, prayed for the preservation of Rome and a delay of the terrible Day of Reckoning. Some of them even wanted to see in the empire an approximation to the millennium and developed what may be considered a rudimentary "Christian Idea of Progress." They based it on the fact that Jesus Christ was born at the time of the foundation of the Roman Empire and the establishment of the Augustan *Pax Romana*. "It was not through human merit," Eusebius of Caesarea (260?– 340? A.D.) writes, "that at no other time but only since the time of Christ most of the nations were under the single rule of the Romans; for the period of his wonderful sojourn among men coincided with the period when the Romans reached their summit under Augustus who was then the first monarch to rule over most of the nations."[12] "Two great powers sprang up fully as out of one stream and they gave peace to all and brought all together to a state of friendship."[13] "Although the object of the Roman empire to unite all nations in one harmonious whole has already been secured to a large degree, it is destined to be still more perfectly attained, even to the final conquest of the ends of the habitable world . . ."[14] So God, Eusebius asserts in exalting Constantine, "gives even here and now the first-fruits as a

---

[12] *Demonstratio Evangelica*, 3, 7, 139, quoted by Theodore E. Mommsen in *St. Augustine and the Christian Idea of Progress. The Background of the City of God*, "Journal of the History of Ideas," Vol. XII, No. 3, p. 360.
[13] *Theophania*, 3, 2, quoted by Mommsen, *op. cit.*, pp. 361 f.
[14] *Praise of Constantine*, 16, 6, quoted by Mommsen, *op. cit.*, pp. 362 f.

pledge of future rewards, thus assuring in some sort immortal hopes to mortal eyes."[15] From these and similar views Prudentius could conclude that "for Christ, who . . . will come soon, the way is open which the universal friendship of our peace under Roman rule has prepared."[16]

But only about seven years later this pronouncement was violently refuted when in 410 A.D. the Visigoth Alaric, a barbarian pagan, conquered Rome, a feat which nobody had ever accomplished before him. The perplexity of the Christian community was just as unprecedented—at no other moment had Christianity been in such jeopardy. The church father Jerome expressed the general dismay: "The whole world has perished in one city."

The situation is in some respects comparable to that of the year 586 B.C., after the Babylonian conquest of Jerusalem. For the second time the fall of a hieratical earthly state has established a spiritual community. In Jerusalem the destruction of a theocratic kingdom had caused the spiritualization of a humanity-oriented tribe: the floating community of the Jewish diaspora. In Rome the downfall of a supra-ethnic hieratical empire has given birth to the spiritual community of the Catholic Church.

---

[15] *Life of Constantine*, 1, 3, 3, quoted by Mommsen, *op. cit.*, p. 360.
[16] *Contra Symmachum*, II.

7

THE MAN WHO RESCUED THE CHRISTIAN COMMUNITY
from the state of confusion and anxiety, its second founder
after Paul, was *Augustine*. His agony, his urge to save his
own and the community's faith, drove his zealous and penetrating mind into the depths of the Christian situation and
brought him to lay bare the latent paradoxes of the Pauline
doctrine. The ineluctable conclusions he was led to implied
a decisive transformation of the doctrine, a stabilization of
the fateful rift between body and spirit, between a divine
and a secular course of events.

Again, at this turning point in human history, we see how
a life experience, a disturbing, indeed shattering experience,
brought forth a concept which in turn incorporated with and
profoundly changed actuality.

The turmoil among Christian minds in the wake of the
fall of Rome threatened to break up the community into a
multitude of wrangling views and sects. There were many
people who believed that the end of the world and the Day
of Reckoning had begun. Others, who had cherished the
idea of a gradual Christian Progress, were groping for a

meaning of the sudden event. And the various Hellenizing heresies—among them those who, under the influence of Origen, maintained, in Christian garb, the pagan cyclic theory—found an easy escape.

Augustine, in his *City of God,* which was initially an apologetic treatise, like the rest of patristic literature, contested all these views. His main argument is crucial to the future development of Christian doctrine; indeed it laid the foundation for the structure of the medieval world. He put an end to all speculations about the end of the world and the advent of the Kingdom of God, speculations which heretofore all theologians, including his own disciple Orosius, had indulged in. That the fall of Rome would spell the beginning of doomsday was shown by Augustine to be a very questionable assumption; there were indications to the contrary, for instance, the barbarians' strange sparing of the Christian sanctuaries. Whether Rome was to be considered the last monarchy before the millennium, he declared unknowable. In all these conjectures which might be disproved by events, he sensed a menace to the faith. Therefore he rejected them categorically with reference to *Acts 1*:7: "It is not for you to know the times or the seasons, which the Father hath put in his own power." With this general prohibition of pondering over dates and circumstances, the Second Coming appeared put off indefinitely, it lost the concrete substance, which it still preserved in the Jews' infinite, yet momentary, expectation of the Kingdom of God on Earth. For in the meantime the split between a purely earthly and a purely spiritual sphere, the diverting of man from his terrestrial footing to "things above," had taken place. More and more had been taken away from life on earth, it had become a worthless shell of the beyond. *This radical spiritualization, de-temporalization of Christian life was the ultimate achievement of Augustine.* Apart from being the heritage of his Platonism and a result of his fierce suppression of his powerful drives and emotions, it offered indeed the only conceivable way to rescue the Christian faith from the incertitude as to a foreseeable millennium.

Such spiritualization of Christian life made it easier for him to invalidate the Christian idea of Progress. No earthly state of peace has ever been achieved, he declared: "There are still wars, wars among nations for supremacy, wars among sects, wars among Jews, pagans, Christians, heretics, and these wars are becoming more frequent."[1] "Is it not true," he asks, "that since the coming of Christ the state of human affairs has been worse than it was before and that human affairs were once much more fortunate than they are now?"[2] Not only had peace on earth failed, but—and this is the consolation he dispensed—it did not even matter whether it was achieved or not. The only peace that matters, he maintained, is the one which, through the grace of God, man finds in himself, by faith and complete surrender of his will. "When man learns that in himself he is nothing and that he has no help from himself, then arms in himself are broken in pieces, then wars in himself are ended."[3] Here a second change, inevitably following from the first, is noticeable: *the shift from general to individual salvation.*

All material progress, then, is for Augustine a delusion and ends up in disillusion. With the same vehemence and cogency, however, he turns against the ancient cyclic theory.

---

[1] *Enarration on Psalm 45,* quoted by Theodore E. Mommsen in *St. Augustine and the Christian Idea of Progress. The Background of the City of God,* "Journal of the History of Ideas," Vol. XII, No. 3, p. 364.
[2] *Enarration on Psalm 136,* quoted by Mommsen, *op. cit.,* pp. 369 ff.
[3] *Enarration on Psalm 45,* quoted by by Mommsen, *op. cit.,* p. 364.

I must not doubt, he says, "that man has never existed before and that he has been originally created at a certain time,"[4] and that God, "while being himself eternal and without beginning, let the times have a definite beginning; and man, whom he had never made before, he has made within time."[5] "Once and for all Christ died for our sins; but rising from the death will die no more . . . and we, after resurrection, shall be with the Lord forever."[6] "Where are the faithful," he asks, "who could bear hearing that, once having arrived, after a life of so many and extreme calamities (if that can be called life which is actually death, so powerful that the love of it makes us fear that death which liberates us from it) . . . in the sight of God, and . . . having entered into bliss . . . by partaking in his immutable immortality . . . they should at some time or other be forced to leave it . . . and be expelled from that eternity, truth and felicity into hellish mortality, shameful foolishness, and abominable misery, where God is abandoned and truth hated . . . and that such a thing happened and will happen again and again interminably . . . ?"[7] But "if the soul, once liberated as it has never been liberated previously, will never again return to misery, then something happens which has never happened before . . . eternal, never ending blissfulness has come to be."[8]

So for Augustine too, the career of man is a unique train of happening, starting with genesis, continuing with the fall, and ending in salvation, a train of happening whose pivotal

[4] *De Civitate Dei*, XII, 16 (according to the arrangement of chapters in the text of the "Corpus Christianorum" edition, 1955).

[5] *Ibid.*, XII, 15.

[6] *Ibid.*, XII, 14.

[7] *Ibid.*, XII: 21.

[8] *Ibid.*

point is the sacrificial deed of the Savior. Of the previous ascent, however, nothing is left in his doctrine. Since the palpable Kingdom of God receded into the mists of an imponderable future, the simultaneous redemption of all humanity dissolved into a multitude of single, personal salvations, in which *individual predestination* began to assume a predominant role.

In original Christianity baptism was in itself equivalent to absolution and salvation, and was a prominent agent in propagation of Christianity. Augustine's doctrine of predestination, however, reached much farther into the depths of human nature and destiny, beyond the common effect of baptism. In his view, the originally homogeneous human race, as personified in Adam, parted, through Cain and Abel, into two opposing lines of descent, exposing and propagating the twofold nature of man, his inclination toward good or evil, toward the spirit or the flesh, toward the will to devotion or the will to destructive self-assertion, toward love and peace or hatred. This division, ultimately deriving from ancient Persian dualism, and prefiguring modern Freudian dualism, was assumed to go back beyond human origins, into the mythical conflict between angels and demons[9]—the apostasy of the bad angels preceded the fall of men.

But this train of thought has even farther-reaching consequences. A division prevails, through initial predestination, among the Christian community itself, even among baptized Christians. The children of Cain and the children of Abel are constitutionally distinguished by love of evil and love of good. Accordingly, the divine community, the *Civitas Dei*, and the earthly community, the *Civitas Terrena*, are inter-

[9] Augustine, *De Genesi ad litteram*, XI, (Migne 34, col. 437).

mingled with each other (*perplexae, corpora permixta*). The earthly community is not identical with a concrete station, it is *terrena not through collective locality, but through individual proclivity*. It is therefore not to be confused with the Roman Empire, pagan or Christian. A person belongs to it not as a member of a group of people on earth, but through his *personal* inclination for matters of the flesh. Étienne Gilson has beautifully translated the *Civitas Terrena* by *cité des fils de la terre*, community of the children of the earth.[10] Correspondingly, the *Civitas Dei* is not simply equivalent to heaven since it includes the bad angels, who essentially belong among the "children of the earth." To Augustine, the two communities have thus a rather mystical meaning. However, the *Civitas Terrena* is the one in which earthly, material happenings can be perceived visually, sensorily—in accordance with the Biblical writing to which Augustine refers "that Cain founded a city, but Abel, being an alien, did not."[11] In contrast, the invisible eternal City of God is seen as the only true community, the only one which may justly be a called a community, because in it justice, peace and love prevail. All this means de-temporalization and de-historization. Upon his individual death the predestined saint enters the beyond of eternal bliss, in which he actually has already dwelt here below as an "alien" on earth; the predestined seeker of the flesh passes into eternal perdition.

Thus, in his effort to rescue Christian faith and Christian unity, Augustine is driven to ever deeper probing into the problems of the Christian situation. His ardent, emotionally

[10] Etienne Gilson, *Les Métamorphoses de la Cité de Dieu* (Louvain-Paris, 1952), p. 55.
[11] *De Civitate Dei*, XV, 1.

charged intellect impelled him to bring fully out into the open the intrinsic paradoxes of the Pauline doctrine, indeed to carry them even further.

We remember that these problems ultimately derive from the Christian reversal of man's relationship to God: God, in his *grace* sent down his son in human form in order to redeem all mankind, through vicarious self-sacrifice, from the bondage of sin and the penalties incurred by the violation of the laws of God. In this way God has released man from the duty actively to contribute to the advent of his kingdom. What brings man salvation is *faith* alone, faith in the mercy of God, and the confirmation of his faith in the magic, sacramental act of *baptism* which since Jewish times has been a ceremony of cleansing from pagan impurity. Redemption through baptism implied that *before* this act *all* human beings were contaminated with sin, for otherwise God's dispensing of grace and Christ's sacrifice would be senseless for the just. This called for the assumption of *original, genetically inherited sinfulness*.[12] Now, according to Paul, the believer was baptized into Christ's death and resurrected in him as a new man; and from then on he is dead to earthly life and in a hidden way living with Christ in the above. This Pauline introduction of baptism as the effective act of salvation already entails a basic doctrinal incompatibility: it was an individual anticipation of the all-embracing Kingdom of God, which, however, was still expected in the near future. It also detracted from the significance of the *Last Judgment*, since the *mercy of God*, as enacted in Christ's sacrifice, and affirmed in the act of faith, was already to have absolved the

[12] Augustine considers every single human being given to sin, not only generally, by Adam's fall and hereditary transmission of concupiscence, but also individually, through his having been conceived in sin.

faithful from his sins. Indeed Paul's emphasis on *grace* carried from the beginning, as we have seen from his reference to God's selection of Jacob, the seeds of the doctrine of *predestination,* and its conflict with Christ's sacrificial salvation of all.

These paradoxes inherent in the Pauline doctrine were greatly sharpened by Augustine. By reaching back beyond baptism and extending God's selection beyond Jacob and Esau to Abel and Cain, indeed to the origin of man, he overstressed the power, but at the same time restricted the effect, of the grace of God. He made omnipotent Grace into a quasi impersonal force of which Jesus Christ was an instrument rather than a loving bestower. He thereby devaluated the crucial deed and the dominant position of Jesus Christ. The doctrine of original predestination was hardly compatible with the doctrine of original sin and of Christ's sacrificial redemption of all mankind; it contradicted the redemptive effect of baptism as an act of faith. Augustine finally narrowed down the actual Christian community to the wholly spiritual City of God which he strictly separated from the life of the flesh.

From these difficulties there emerged as the only possible compromise the institution of the *Catholic Church* as a spatially as well as temporally mediative instance, as an earthly substitute for the City of God, and indefinitely provisional realization of the Kingdom of God, which had failed to appear. The City of God, represented by the church, replaced the Kingdom of God. Under the influence of Augustine the notion gradually prevailed that with the growing power of the church the Kingdom of God had actually begun.[13] The intercession of the exalted church with her

[13] Cf. Ernst Bernheim, *Mittelalterliche Zeitanschanungen* (Tübingen, 1918), pp. 67 f.

sacramental services and her magical power of absolution made it possible to reintroduce in manifold casuistic gradations a certain influence of personal merit on salvation. Since nobody knew whether he was predestined to salvation, people sought refuge in the objective effects of sacramental acts and in the mediating offices of the church which had seized the administration of Christ's loving mercy.

Since, in Augustine's view, the will of man is subject to divine grace, which works through predestination and sacramental acts, since man is prevented from all active, or even speculative participation in the advent of the Kingdom of God, arrested as he is in his faith and his powerless uncertainty—for even the godly life of the righteous has come to be a mere function of faith, a deadening to actual life—the career of man has again become a circular course, although to be sure, a *unique circular course*. Man, constitutionally sinful through Adam's fall, genetically divided, through original predestination, into Abel and Cain, into providentially salvable and damnable human beings, returns individually, if so predestined, into the heavenly bliss for which he was initially created. The whole process of developing consciousness and of conscious striving toward worldly perfection, the process which had started human history, is eliminated in Augustine's doctrine. What was left in it of this matured consciousness was man's "gradual ascent from the temporal to a grasp of the eternal, and from the visible to the invisible."[14]

This tendency of Augustine's to devaluate history was reinforced by his preoccupation with *the nature of time*, which had arisen as a consequence of the fundamental division between the bodily and the spiritual spheres. Since for him the road to salvation no longer leads through happenings on

[14] *De Civitate Dei*, X, 14.

79

earth, but takes its course on a spiritual level—or, in effect, does not take a course at all, being predestined from the outset—Augustine was bound to arrive at a concept of time exactly opposite to that of original Christianity, an extremely problematic concept whose incongruities he was never able to overcome. For the early Christians the history of salvation was still naively identified with the process of human history proper. It moved "in time" toward the concretely expected Kingdom of God on earth, and divine "eternity" was nothing other than infinite time, in which the measurable time of man was imbedded. To be sure, the "above," the "hidden life" *in Christo* was introduced by Paul, but this hidden life of the faithful was at that point a mere temporizing until at some early date the Kingdom of God would materialize in which heaven and earth were expected to fuse. With Augustine the emphasis shifted radically to the spiritual sphere, whereby the whole aspect of relationships was reversed, and the nature of time became an insoluble problem. Time now was the terrestrial opposite to purely spiritual eternity, i.e. *timelessness,* in which God resides. Time became a thing, a material abstract, equal to other things, which, all of them, were created by God. And this "material" character of time caused the perplexity with which Augustine struggled: "How could innumerable ages pass over," he writes, "which thyself (God Omnipotent, All-creator and . . . Maker of heaven and earth) hadst not made; thou being the author and creator of all ages? Or what times should these have been, which were not made by thee? Or, how should they pass over, if so be they never were?"[15] The assumption that God was the creator of time met with particular difficulties when it faced a question fre-

---

[15] *Confessiones,* XI, 13.

quently asked in those days: What did God do, what was his condition before he started creating? "Seeing therefore thou art the Creator of all times; if any time had passed before thou madest heaven and earth, why then is it said, that thou didst forbear to work? For that very time hadst thou made; nor could there any times pass over, before thou hadst made times. But if before heaven and earth there were no time, why is it then demanded, what thou didst? For there was no THEN, whenas there was no time. Nor dost thou in time precede times; else thou shouldest not precede all times. But thou precedest all times past, by high advantage of an ever present eternity; and thou goest beyond all times to come even because they are to come, and when they shall come, they shall be past; whereas thou art still the same. . . . Thy years neither go nor come; whereas these years of ours do both go and come; that in their order they may all come. Thy years stand all at once, because they stand . . . but these years of thine shall all be ours, when all time shall cease to be."[16] "In no time therefore, hadst thou 'not made' anything: because very time itself was of thy making: and there be no times coeternal with thee, for that thou still remainest the same; but should they still remain, verily they should not be times. For what is time? Who is able easily and briefly to explain that?" The conclusion of all this is the complete futility, indeed non-entity of time: "Those two times . . . , past and to come, in what sort are they, seeing the past is now no longer, and that to come is not yet? As for the present, should it always be present and never pass into times past, verily it should not be time but eternity. If then time present, to be time, only comes into existence because it passeth into time past; how can we say that also to be, whose

[16] *Confessiones*, XI, 13.

cause of being is, that it shall not be: that we cannot, forsooth, affirm that time is, but only because it is tending not to be? *(due ergo illa tempora, praeteritum et futurum, quomodo sunt, quando et praeteritum iam non est et futurum nondum est? praesens autem si semper esset praesens, nec in praeteritum transiret, non tam esset tempus, sed aeternitas. si ergo praesens, ut tempus sit, ideo fit, quia in praeteritum transit, quomodo et hoc esse dicimus, cui causa, ut sit, illa est, quia non erit, ut scilicet non vere dicamus tempus esse, nisi quia tendit non esse?)*"[17]

In *De Civitate Dei* Augustine says: ". . . where there is no creature whose changes and movements constitute time, there can be no time at all. . . . Time, however, consisting of change as it does cannot be coeval with immutable eternity."[18]

In this connection Augustine gets entangled in unsolvable difficulties when it comes to the special temporal status of the angels, who play a prominent role in his system. (The rebellion of some of the angels was supposed to have caused the creation of man: the elect among humans were believed intended by God to replace the angelic apostates in the spiritual company of God.) Since God, he argues, has always been the Lord, he must have had always subjects who were created by him out of nothing and cannot be co-eternal with him. These subject beings are, before the creation of man, the angels who, although created by him, have always existed with him. So, "although the immortality of the angels does not take place in time nor has passed in time, nor is it apt to come in a future, their movements [for instance the rebellion of some of them] still pass over from

[17] *Confessiones,* XI, 14.
[18] *De Civitate Dei,* XII, 16.

past to future and therefore they cannot be coeternal with their creator of whom it cannot be said that in his existence there was anything which no longer is or is not yet."[19] Thus, Augustine was forced to assume degrees of eternity initiating the later, most important distinction between three temporal spheres, divine eternity *(aeternitas)*, human time *(tempus)*, and in between the two the *"aevum,"* the dimension of the wholly spiritual beings who were created, but immortal, "eviternal." Augustine himself, however, frankly admitted that how this can be, that God was before his creations, but never without them, this possibility "is beyond the capacities of my understanding."

Time, then, the sphere of human life, is earthly and futile, it is essentially non-being. In this view we may find traces of Augustine's original Greekness and Platonism. With the Greeks, however, the cyclically recurrent earthly time-span of man had been a replica of divine or cosmic immutability. For Augustine the unique time of man on earth has become entirely worthless and chaotic. "As to the time of the mortals," he writes, "which lasts a few days and finds its end, what does it matter under what rule a man destined to death lives. . . . What difference it can make to the welfare and good conduct, in which the true nobility of man consists, whether some have conquered and others were defeated, this I do not see, not to speak of that idle pride in human glory. . . ."[20]

So what happened on earth, the place of the *Civitas Terrena,* is of no importance to Augustine. What concerns him is alone the *Civitas Dei,* and this community has indeed an evolution, which, however, consists solely in the process of

[19] *Ibid.,*
[20] *De Civitate Dei,* V, 17.

God's creation. This evolutional road of the *Civitas Dei* is, according to its purely spiritual nature, no longer traditionally divided into the sequence of the four or five earthly monarchies, but, according to a more recent custom, into seven periods representing the seven days of creation, whereby the earthly changes are just a reflection or accompaniment of Biblical history. The first day lasts from Adam to the Flood, the second from the Flood to Abraham (both reckoned in terms not of time, but of generations, each of them comprising ten generations). They are followed by three periods, or days of God, of fourteen generations each: from Abraham to David, from David to the Babylonian Captivity, and from there to the birth of Christ. The sixth period is Augustine's own, the generations of which must not, and cannot, be measured. And finally, on the seventh day God will rest. "That seventh day . . . will be our Sabbath whose end will not be evening, but the Day of the Lord. . . ."[21] In it the organic circle closes. Something happens which has never happened before: eternal, never-ending bliss sets in. But what appears here to be new consists solely, as stated before, in man's newly acquired consciousness of the miserable state of mortality, a wholly inactive, unproductive consciousness. "As far as the enjoyment of the present bliss is concerned, the first man in Paradise was happier than any righteous man in this state of mortal infirmity. But regarding the hopeful expectation of future bliss, anybody in any, and even the worst, physical pains, if only he can be sure, not on the basis of mere supposition, but confirmed by true certitude, that he ultimately will be free of all discomfort and will in the company of angels forever enjoy the presence of the supreme God—this man is

[21] *De Civitate Dei,* XXII, 30.

more blessed than that pristine man, who even in that great felicity of Paradise, was still uncertain about his Fall."[22]

But who could, here below, be absolutely certain about his future bliss? "[Even the faithful] who may be sure of the reward of their steadfastness, can by no means be certain of their perseverance. For who could know that he will persevere in his righteous conduct to the end, unless he is granted assurance, through some revelation, by him who, in his just and concealed judgment, though deceiving none, does not inform everybody,"[23] man's very perseverance being preordained. Thus, one uncertainty is counterbalanced by another. Only the ultimate bliss in the beyond exceeds the pristine bliss in Paradise, by the certainty, the consciousness of eternity.

Augustine himself seems to have felt the precariousness of this gain from bliss to bliss, a perplexity which renders the whole of God's design for human destiny, including Christ's sacrifice, highly questionable. He makes two ineffectual attempts to excogitate an advantage of the final over the primal bliss. Both attempts struggle with the same incompatibilities inherent in the doctrine of grace and predestination. "The animal body which, according to the apostle, was Adam's, was not created such that he could not under any circumstances die, but that he could not die if he had not sinned. . . . Those men, however, who are elected by the grace of God to belong among the fellow-citizens of the holy angels abiding forever in the blessed life, are endowed with spiritual bodies of such a kind that they can never more either sin or die."[24] In his second at-

[22] *De Civitate Dei,* XI, 12.
[23] *Ibid.*
[24] *De Civitate Dei,* XXII, 30.

tempt, the desperate sophistry of his reasoning resorts to a linguistic device: "the first free will which was given to man when he was created upright was *able not to sin,* but *also to sin;* this ultimate [freedom of will], however, will be more powerful inasmuch as he will *not be able to sin* [this too indeed by a gift of God, not by virtue of his nature] . . . Just as the original immortality, which Adam lost through his sin, consisted in his *being able not to die,* while the ultimate immortality will consist in his *not being able to die,* so the first free will was such that he *could not sin,* the ultimate will be such that *sin he cannot (sicut prima immortalitas fuit . . . posse non mori, novissima erit non posse mori; ita primum liberum arbitrium posse non peccare, novissium non posse peccare.)*"[25]

It is difficult enough to comprehend how God could initially grant the human being—in Adam—free will to sin or not to sin and then grant those who are elected the ultimate bliss, by dint of sheer grace. But to assume that God would finally endow man with a "free will" which by divine grace is made *incapable* of sinning, is a concept of contortive absurdity. Where there is no choice, there is no free will.

The Old Testament recounts a happening which, in its mythical simplicity, signifies a profound and consistent verity: Man is initially endowed with the capability to disobey, to sin, which means to choose. Man's assertion of free will is the foundation of his actual humanity; it implies consciousness—and consequently suffering, travail, and shame—but also the aspiration to the likeness of God and God's creativity. God's anger at the arrogance of consciousness is tempered in his covenant with the faithful and his command to atone for this arrogance by fulfilling and bring-

[25] *Ibid.*

86

ing to perfection man's potential humanity and Godlikeness through sanctification of life and conscious preparation for the Kingdom of God on Earth.

This original Biblical concept, as generated by the experiences of the people of Israel, marks, as we have seen, the first realization of a unique destiny of mankind as a whole, that is, of history.

The aim of my account so far has been to show the gapless "chain interaction" of events and concepts, leading from the original Biblical story and its earthly commitment of man up to the extremely sophisticated arguments of Augustine with their paralyzation of human will, their reduction of human consciousness, their invalidation of earthly life and processes, therefore of history, and radical separation of the spiritual and the terrestrial. Intellectually complex and twisted as Augustine's doctrine is, it had an illimitable and very real influence on the foundation and formation of medieval life. Augustine instituted the church as a mediatory terrestrial substitute of the City of God, he established it as a theocratic power claiming supremacy over secular powers, and he thereby inaugurated the millennial contest between the *Regnum* and the *Sacerdotium*. By his interpretation of Luke *14*:23, the so-called *Coge intrare*, he helped make the church increasingly militant, and in this way contributed to its crusades and their offshoot, the Inquisition. And far beyond the medieval centuries the influence of his doctrine of predestination reached with renewed vigor into the anticlerical reforms of Luther and Calvin, and the immeasurable effects of Puritanism.

Apart from this influence on the actual course of events, Augustine has certainly a special place in the formation of historical thought. To be sure, he was not what he was long considered to be, the inaugurator of "philosophy of history." His concern was not with history, but with the workings of God's creation. Indeed he invalidated the very medium of history, which is time. However, objectively, involuntarily, he was the first to set up an intellectual framework for the contemplation of the destiny of man. And his parting of eternity and time, his inconclusive struggles with the problem of time and the controversies it aroused, in fact, his sharp separation of spirit and body, gave the decisive impulse to the final emancipation of the process of history. He may be seen as *the initiator of the secularization of man.*

8

HISTORY, INDEED LIFE AS A WHOLE, PROCEEDS IN tides. Waves advance to fullest capacity, then recede, to advance till farther, *reculent pour mieux sauter*. But even in recession, gains are not wiped out. Anything that once has come into existence can no longer vanish completely; it may be obscured, suppressed, pushed into the background for a time, it may settle into fusion with other movements; but eventually it will reappear, in a new guise and with redoubled force.

So, in the Middle Ages, the church, firmly established with the help of Augustine as the transition to the City of God and as a mediating, alleviating power, destined to direct the conduct of man, made life on earth provisionally possible and absolvable in ever proliferating degrees; indeed, the church as an organizing force furthered earthly life in many ways. Life on earth went on, and with it disputes, conflicts, compromises. But underneath, through monasticism and individual saints, mortification of the flesh and hidden life in the above continued; and still, in situations of extreme stress a sense of the imminence of the Day of

Judgment and the Millennium welled up anew, and the expectation, though mostly dormant, persisted for a long time. At any rate, life remained stringently determined by the stable role of religious absolutes.

Yet, *the split between spirit and body*, once established, was bound to promote the ascendancy of pressing material concerns. The stir of independent mundane developments —the emancipation of secular history, actual and conceptual—made itself felt with ever increasing force.

With Augustine and his invalidation of time, human history seemed arrested, and for a certain time, in the actual "Dark Ages" (the seventh and eighth centuries), it really appeared the way Augustine had pictured it: a chaotic medley of events, a senseless up and down of futile powers. But soon afterwards, it began to take definite shape and to move ahead in the direction of secular emancipation. Again, we find a multiple conjunction and chain interaction of agents, spiritual and material, working toward this growing predominance of human time, that is to say, of secular history.

It started with the expanding Christianization of the Germanic tribes, and the concomitant barbarian conquest of the terrestrial part of the Roman Empire. At first, the Germanic rulers followed, and had to follow, the organizational guidance of the ecclesiastical remnant of the Imperium. But the inevitable antagonisms ensuing from these interconnected events bore paradoxical results: the contest between the secular and the spiritual dominion drove the latter into a more and more material self-assertion. The Curia, the *sacerdotium* itself, increasingly indulged in political affairs and was lured into mundane aspirations and ostentatious self-gratifications. And in the militant encounter with the infidels, which combined missionary and expansionist aims, the very conflicts engendered contacts and counterinfluences.

Pope Leo III made Charlemagne Roman Emperor, Christianization gave rise to the wars against the Spanish and South-Italian Saracens, which preluded and accompanied the Crusades. This is where the companion streak of human history, the Islamic, comes in as a counterpart and stimulus to the main, Western movement, the only one ultimately to lead to the latest—scientific, industrial, and technological —stage of humanity. The fight against the Moslems reopened the Mediterranean not only as a medium for the transmission of pre-Christian knowledge, but also as an arena of international trade and the attendant economic activities in which, together with the worldly powers, the temporalized papacy engaged. Propagation of the faith was a welcome support and pretense for the innate lust for adventure and booty, which incited seafarers to the exploration of new regions, making use of, and in turn, encouraging, scientific innovations[1] as well as expanding commerce.

I cannot and I need not, in our context, describe in detail the complex interaction of all these factors fostering secularization. It must suffice to single out the evolutionary strains which are foremost in emancipating secular history, and fundamentally transforming human consciousness. We begin with the one that leads to the ascendancy of pure reason and the development of science and technology.

This trend begins within the *theological domain*. In the first centuries A.D. Christian teachings had still been emotionally fluid; doctrines were not as yet fixed dogmas. The turbulent Hellenistic era teemed with syncretistic sects, Gnostics, Montanists, Donatists, Marcionites, Manichaeans,

[1] The Portuguese prince Henry the Navigator for instance prepared his voyages by founding the first observatory.

followers of Arius, and others. Partly related with the Pauline doctrine, and competing with it, they moved in and out of Christian communities, sporadically accepted and rejected. Even the Arian controversy, concerning Christ's homogeneity *(homoousía)* with God, which appeared settled at the Council of Nicaea (325), flared up again under the emperors Constantius, Valens, and Julianus, until the Athanasian concept of homogeneity, which together with the homogeneity of the Holy Ghost constituted the *Holy Trinity,* became finally dogmatized at the Synod of Constantinople in 381. What occupied and disturbed the minds of this period, was mainly the Christological problem: whether Christ was substantially one with God—who, however, could hardly be imagined as a composite being—or whether he was created by God in the same way the world was created by him; in other words, whether Christ was spiritually begotten, or created, whether he was an inalienable part of God, or a kind of demigod whose power was occasioned and restricted. Already here the problem of time began to loom, which later troubled Augustine so deeply.[2]

When, after the "dark" centuries, the theological controversies started again, their character had changed fundamentally. While patristic literature had been primarily apologetic and externally polemic, scholasticism delved more profoundly—in the manner of Augustine, who marked an end and a beginning—and more and more rationally into the philosophical problems of the religious tenets.

[2] The doctrine of the divine nature, i.e. of an eternal, ever-repeated generation, of the Son was compatible with Origen's cyclic view of an ever-recurrent creation of the world, but incompatible with the Biblical assumption of the uniqueness of the human process. The Arian doctrine of the creation of Christ in time, just as the whole world has been created in time, made him a merely temporal power. The precarious resolution of this conflict remained for Augustine.

This change, again, was due to a conflux of diverse circumstances, all of them deriving from the one preceding historical process.

First of all, the progressive Christianization of the Celtic and Germanic tribes, which followed the Germanic inheritance of the Christianized Roman Empire, shifted the focus of events to the Northern peoples and drew fresh forces into the Christian orbit. These new forces, Anglo-Saxon, Irish, Frankish (later French) were not as thoroughly Christianized as those which originally had formed Christianity, and which, having grown out of its manifold Oriental and classical traditions, had been profoundly familiar with them. Even when, in certain circumstances, these Nordic missionaries became acquainted with the old theological problems, they were scarcely prepared to deal with them, and their approach to the Christian faith was in general one of naïve piety and tough, practical zeal, a sense of factuality and immediate experience. The first of the various "renaissances" which were brought to the fore by recent historical studies, the "Carolingian Renaissance," was characterized by a remarkable pragmatic soberness, indeed an early form of rationalism. Charlemagne, with all his Christian campaigning and destruction of pagan sanctuaries, shows, even in ecclesiastical matters, a cool-headed, unswerving attention to his political interests which made some historians call him downright irreligious.

The early philosophical controversies arising in the ninth century from the study of the Scriptures—such as the dispute between the abbot of Tours, Fridugise (*Fredegisus*) and Agobard of Lyon on the reality or irreality of the nothingness and darkness from which God had created the world—give evidence of the clumsy use of a troubled common sense; the distinction between *ratio* and *auctoritas* (reason and authority) appears for the first time. A Biblical or theological assertion must be confirmed, so it is said in Fridugise's treatise *De nihilo et tenebris,* first rationally and then authoritatively, that is, on grounds of ecclesiastical authority; but even this authority must be rational.[3] Here, a linguistic tautology of reason and authority is still assumed, and the later scholastic conflict is avoided: in saying that nothingness *is* nothing, the simple use of the predicate "to be" is supposed to prove that nothingness is something. This naive argument is based on the notion that God had imparted names to his creations, so that everything may be recognized by its name. There is no thing without the word that belongs to it, and accordingly no word without a thing which it is to designate.

What appears even more noteworthy than the explicit contraposition of *ratio* and *auctoritas* is the need to explain and corroborate Biblical history rationally, to support faith with reason. This will ultimately, in the eleventh century, impel Anselm of Canterbury to prove rationally the very existence of God, although for him faith is still the prerequisite of rational understanding: *Credo ut intelligam,* I believe in order to understand. But long before him the Irishman Johannes Scotus Erigena, the philosophical genius of the ninth century, asserted the *autonomy,* indeed the *supremacy of reason.* In his view, the authority of the Fathers is authority only because, being by no means suprarational, it stands the test of reason.

Such unencumbered inclination toward common sense

[3] *primum ratione, in quantum hominis ratio patitur* (as far as human reason reaches), *deinde auctoritate non qualibet sed rationali duntaxat* (if properly considered).

and reason was brought by the Northern scholars to the great problems of Christian doctrine: *the problem of transsubstantiation,* i.e. the question as to how in the process of communion bread and wine can be transformed into the body and blood of Jesus Christ when the accidental qualities—color, taste, palpability—subsist; the problem of the *unity of trinity,* and, in connection with it, the problem of the *reality or irreality of universals,* that is, *of genera and species.* In the first controversy, which took place in the eleventh century, Bérenger, head of the Cathedral School of Tours, was the champion of reason and empirical evidence. Although transsubstantiation did not become an official Catholic dogma until 1215, Bérenger's attack was considered heretical even in his own time; he exposed the rational vulnerability of the dogma before its actual proclamation. The controversy about universals was, however, much more incisive and decisive in regard to the progress of secularization.

For in the meantime another development had come to the support of the rational forces: a radical shift in the character of pagan influence on Christian thought. Such influence had been strong from the beginning of the Christian era, with considerable effect on Paul himself and on the Church Fathers. The fullness of Greek thinking had been present at the formation of the new religion and had contributed to it in many ways. But what in Greek philosophy had been conducive and somewhat akin (even when antagonistic) to Christianism in its formative phase were supranatural and suprarational movements: Stoicism, Platonism, particularly in its late derivations, Jewish Alexandrianism (Philo), Neoplatonism, Neo-Pythagoreanism, and the like. Aristotle was left aside, was indeed in ill repute, especially his logic, which even Augustine considered of no value, "not serving to any good employment, but to my destruction rather."[4]

But, as is well-known, in the Middle Ages it was precisely Aristotle who gradually came to predominate over Plato—although Neoplatonism continued to be influential in scholastic philosophy and often blended with Aristotelian theories—and precisely Aristotle's logic, or, as it was later called, dialectic, became a powerful vehicle for the promotion of reason. This was due to the fact that among the debris of ancient texts, which emerged from the destructive turmoil of the dark centuries, Aristotle's logic had been carried over as an isolated part of his writings, a section which was considered a mere instrument *(organon)* for training the mind. It is an intricate and fascinating story, how, thanks to a Neoplatonist fragment, Porphyry's introduction *(Isagōgē)* to Aristotle's categories, or rather a Latin translation of it, with commentary, by the Roman statesman and scholar, Boethius, Aristotle's logic not only survived the dark period, but assumed tremendous importance. To exert such influence, it had to be such specific fragment. For, while the bulk of Aristotle's work, had it been known at the time, would still have been rejected by the dominant church authorities, his logic as a purely functional tool could become an accepted part of the "liberal arts" which had passed from decaying antiquity into ecclesiastical use. The "instrument" of Aristotle's logic actually did sharpen the schoolmen's minds for a more and more rational, critical look at the fundamentals of Christian doctrine. Indeed, Porphyry's *Isagōgē* brought to the fore that momentous philosophical problem inherent in the basic divergence of Platonic and

[4] *Confessiones,* IV, 16.

Aristotelian thought, which in the eleventh century became the central theme of scholastic controversy: *the problem of the universals,* that is, the question whether genera and species are absolute *realities*—hence divinely established absolutes—or whether they are just common *names (nomina, voces)* inferred and invented by the human mind—hence products of reasoning. The nominalists, in the end, carried their cause, not only against the realists, but implicitly for the rise of rationalism and science.

Militant Christianity extended contacts with the Moslems, which had inestimable effects on Western thoughts, through an ever waxing influx of ancient texts. In the eleventh century the Christian Normans conquered Southern Italy and Sicily from the Saracens. The Christian reconquest of Spain took place at approximately the same time, from the eleventh to the twelfth century. A flow of transmission of ancient knowledge and thinking followed this opening of long-closed gates. Among the various sources of such communication those of the Iberian peninsula were the most important. Spain, Charles Homer Haskins says, "has its romance of commerce, from the 'corded bales' of the Tyrian trader to the silver fleets of the Indies; of discovery and conquest, as personified in Columbus and the conquistadores; of crusading and knight errantry in the Cid and Don Quixote. It has also its romance of scholarship, of adventure in new paths of learning and even in forbidden bypaths. In consequence of the Saracen conquest, the Peninsula became for the greater portion of the Middle Ages a part of the Mohammedan East, heir to its learning and its science, . . . and the principal means of their introduction into Western Europe. When, in the twelfth century, the Latin world began to absorb this Oriental lore, the pioneers of the new learning turned chiefly to Spain, where one after another sought the key to knowledge in the mathematics and astronomy, the astrology and medicine and philosophy which were there stored up. . . . The great adventure of the European scholar lay in the Peninsula."[5] This "lure of Spain" began to become really active only in the wake of the advance of the Christian armies, that is, in the twelfth century.

While in the Eastern (Byzantine) Empire the Greek tradition was never lost, it hardly transpired into the West in the early Middle Ages. But "the learning of the Greeks spread widely to the eastward by translation into Syriac, Hebrew, and Arabic . . . these versions sometimes preserving works of which the Greek originals have been lost. . . . The Semitic versions . . . are of the greatest importance for the West, constituting as they did the chief vehicle for the transmission of Greek science and philosophy to Latin Europe, together with the additions which had been made en route. The route was at times long and devious, from Greek into Syriac or Hebrew, thence into Arabic and thence into Latin, often with Spanish as an intermediary, but it was much travelled and led at last to the Latin West."[6] The translating and commenting mediators, in Spain itself and in Southern France into which the movement first expanded, were mostly Jews.

What concerns us here is the introduction of the whole body of Aristotelian philosophy into Christian thought, and the revolutionary effect which it carried, particularly since the texts were accompanied by commentaries of Arab and Jewish scholars and, at first, transmitted in the version given

[5] Charles H. Haskins, *The Renaissance of the Twelfth Century* (Cambridge, Mass., 1927; New York: Meridian Books), Chap. IX.
[6] *Ibid.*

to them by the great Arab philosopher Averroës (1126–1198). This acute thinker and extreme Aristotelian had already come into conflict with his own Islamic religion which relished certain Aristotelian theories no more than did Judaism and Christianity. Under the stress of this conflict, Averroës sought a solution, or rather escape, in differentiating between a literal, popularly religious, and an allegorical, i.e. philosophical, interpretation of the Koran. For him, only *reason* would be able to decide which parts are genuine religious tradition and which of the dogmas must be interpreted and how they must be interpreted. In this sense, Averroës is the actual founder of the *doctrine of double truth*, which was later explicitly proclaimed by his French disciple Siger de Brabant. It meant that something can be true in religion, but false in philosophy, and vice versa. This doctrine created a basically incurable *split between reason and faith*. It spelled *the beginning of the triumph of reason*.

Actually, the philosophy of Aristotle contained elements useful to both of the contending scholastic parties, the realists and the nominalists. This, aside from the fascination of dialectic, appears to be the reason why Aristotelianism exerted such authoritative power over the medieval minds that the basic controversies were couched in Aristotelian terms: On the one hand, Aristotle's God is the sole, purely spiritual, immaterial substance, the motionless mover and end, the unity and creative nature of all things; and the genera—secondary substances—are in themselves real; this was apt to please the realists. On the other hand, however, the genera *are not independent* realities, they actually exist and can be comprehended only *in* the things which are many and manifold. The genera are the forming principles, and as such the moving causes and ultimate ends, of material potentialities. Hence they are tied up with individual entities; and while, *metaphysically*, as originative, formative substances, the genera are *first*, they are *logically and temporally last*, because we can grasp them only by means of inductively reached concepts. And this was amenable to a nominalist interpretation.

There were, to be sure, certain points in Aristotle's theory, particularly as emphasized by Averroës, which fundamentally contradicted Christian doctrines and shocked the church authorities at first into a prohibition of the Aristotelian philosophy; the prohibition was ineffectual and short-lived. One of the critical points was Aristotle's denial of the immortality of the individual soul; the other, somehow connected with the first, but more important in our context, was the problem of *time*, its divine creation or coeternity—the old Augustinian dilemma, whose scope and implications were now fully revealed through the confrontation of the Christian doctrine with the Aristotelian theory and the meanwhile refined dialectic analysis.

But soon the Aristotelian distinction and relation of form and matter, their division and junction, proved useful in easing the dilemma; and the new expedient of the double truth, and the widening separation of theology and philosophy relieved it even more—even when, as in the case of Thomas Aquinas, a strict contradiction of reason and faith was denied.

Augustine's quandary derived from his still naïvely treating time as a material thing, on a par with other things belonging to the degraded world. Now, as a result of Aristotelian training, the problem of creation, or infinity, of time became identical with the general problem of matter; and matter, through its "marriage" with spiritual form, indeed its potentiality of accepting form, and tendency toward form, assumed some part in divine creation and became subject to subtle distinctions (a general *"materia prima"* and a physically shaped *"materia secunda"* or *"signata,"* a perceptible *"materia sensibilis"* and a merely thinkable *"materia intelligibilis"*). Time was connected with causation, causation with creation: if, as Bonaventura and Thomas Aquinas argued, every finite being is caused by another such being, the chain of caused beings must ultimately lead back to a primal *uncaused being,* a *causa prima,* accordingly to *creation,* and, on the other hand, if creation is accepted on the ground of faith, then it follows that the world had a beginning. It was, however, also considered that the divine act of creation, or creative mediation, may be eternal *(creatio continua),* and so also may be its result, the world, i.e. matter, i.e. time. The problem that had led Augustine into a personally insuperable impasse, was now made tolerable, or almost resolvable, by its dispersal into multiple, distinct, and more and more abstract problems, and, particularly, by the possibility of shifting their resolution conveniently to and fro, from revelation to philosophy, and from logic to faith.

The final victory of reason over faith, which meant the supremacy of plainly secular, historical time over sheer spiritual sempiternity—and, implicitly, the precondition of empirical science—was brought about by the establishment of the *exclusive reality of individual things.* Aristotle had laid the foundation, and Bonaventura (1221–1274), in his train, saw individuality arising from the conjunction of matter and form. Thomas Aquinas (1225–1274), actually anticipated the underlying principle of modern science: Although knowledge is concerned with the universals—we would say "laws"—*(scientia est universalium)*, these universals, being immanent in the individual things, can only be derived from them through abstraction *(universale fit per abstractionem a materia individuali)*. The intellect apprehends the universals, i.e. essentials, by singling them out from the individual entities in which they inhere, but they do not themselves have a separate, independent existence, in fact they have essence, but not existence *(universalia . . . non sunt res subsistentes, sed habent esse solum in singularibus)*. Duns Scotus (1265, or 1272–1308) did away with the distinction between essence and existence: for him, all that exists is *eo ipso*, by its very existence, essential, and therefore to be considered universal. But beyond the essentiality of all being, he recognizes in single things an additional special quality of *sheer individuality*, of precise *thisness (haecceitas)*. Such concepts paved the way for the radical nominalism of Petrus Auriolus (around 1300), a disciple of Duns Scotus, Durand de Saint-Pourçain, and finally William of Ockham (born around 1300, died 1349), for whom *only individual entities exist in reality*. Their scepticism extended to all metaphysical speculation, and severed most sharply faith from logical thought, for which complete freedom was demanded. Ockham went so far as to question the conclusion, that a series of finite causes must ultimately lead to God as a *prima causa*, and even to deny that the unity and infinity of God can be demonstrated; a plurality of worlds and creators seemed to him conceivable.

The Ockhamist school in Paris became the center of scientific movements breaking through the barriers of scholastic and Aristotelian authority: from the fourteenth century on, a school of *Moderni* (the *Nominales*) stood opposed to a school of *Antiqui* (the *Reales*). Innovations of great consequence originated here and radiated into Germany and Italy. Jean Buridan, Albert of Saxony, Nicholas of Oresme were the actual initiators of modern dynamics, celestial mechanics, and analytical geometry, the precursors of Copernicus and Galileo.

Significantly, these innovations proceeded from the theory of impetus, that is, from the problem of motion. The change is most lucidly described by Herbert Butterfield in his essay on the *Historical Importance of a Theory of Impetus:* According to the Aristotelian theory "a body would keep in movement only so long as a mover was actually in contact with it, imparting motion to it all the time. . . . [in the] Aristotelian universe . . . the things that were in motion had to be accompanied by a mover all the time . . . it was a universe in which unseen hands had to be in constant operation, and sublime Intelligences had to roll the planetary spheres around. Alternatively, bodies had to be endowed with souls and aspirations . . . so that matter itself seemed to possess mystical qualities . . . the modern theory of motion is the great factor which in the seventeenth century helped to drive the spirits out of the world and opened a way to a universe that ran like a piece of clockwork. Not only so—but the very first men who in the middle ages launched the great attack on the Aristotelian theory were conscious of the fact that this colossal issue was involved in the question. The first of the important figures, Jean Buridan, in the middle of the fourteenth century pointed out that his alternative interpretation would eliminate the need for the Intelligences that turned the celestial spheres. . . . Not much later than this, Nicolas of Oresme went farther still, and said that on the new alternative theory God

103

might have started off the universe as a kind of clock and left it to run of itself. . . . Here we have a case of a consistent body of teaching carried on and developed as a tradition by a school of thinkers, particularly in Paris, and still being taught in Paris at the beginning of the sixteenth century. It has a continuous history—we know how this teaching passed into Italy . . . how Leonardo da Vinci picked it up . . . and how some of what were once considered to be remarkable strokes of modernity, remarkable flashes of genius, in his notebooks, were in reality transcriptions from fourteenth-century Parisian scholastic writers. We know how the teaching gained a foothold in later sixteenth-century Italy, amongst the men who influenced Galileo . . . and how the early writings of Galileo on motion belonged precisely to this school of teaching."[7]

A marked disposition toward nature, more prevalent among the Northern peoples, began developing methodically even in the twelfth and thirteenth centuries. Stimulated as it was by Aristotelian and Neoplatonic thought, it went beyond it with independent observation, experimentation, and mathematical application. Scholars like Robert Grosseteste, Petrus Peregrinus of Maricourt (whom Roger Bacon called *dominus experimentorum et experimentator fidelis*), Albertus Magnus, Witelo, Dietrich of Freiberg, and Roger Bacon—not to forget the emperor Frederick II— highlight the stages of this increasing gravitation toward life on earth. Albertus (1193?–1280) explicitly indicated the rules of modern scientific proceeding: "Of those things . . ." he remarked, "we accept as certain, some we have ourselves verified by experiment *(experimento probavimus)*, but some

[7] Herbert Butterfield, *The Origins of Modern Science* (New York, 1952), pp. 3, 6 f.

we derive from the words of people of whom we have good knowledge, but not from facile words *(non de facili aliqua diceret)*, only from those which are proved by experiment."[8] And Roger Bacon counts his teacher, Robert Grosseteste (1175–1253) reverently among those "most renowned men who, by means of the powerful command of mathematics, have been able to explain the causes of all things."[9] Hence, the *principles and prerequisites of modern science:* the *sole reality of individual, sensorily graspable entities,* the *method of abstraction,* the *rules of strict, material causality and experimental verification,* and the *means of mathematical expression,* were explicitly formulated even in the twelfth and thirteenth centuries.

The Ockhamists finally tore scholasticism apart by, on the one hand, setting free reason, experience, and observation, and, on the other hand, driving back religious reformers like Luther and Calvin to pure, dialectically undisturbed devotion to faith and grace. But these reform movements led on their part to secularization, one to the autonomy of the state, the other to the autonomy of business.

[8] Ueberweg-Baumgartner, *Grundriss der Geschichte der Philosophie der patristischen und scholastischen Zeit* (Berlin, 1915), p. 469.
[9] Ueberweg-Baumgartner, *op. cit.,* p. 425.

9

THE RATIONALIZING INFLUENCE OF ARISTOTLE, DOMinant as it came to be, was only one of the many forces driving toward secularization. Even within scholasticism the opposing Neoplatonic trend, mingling and interacting with Aristotelian thought, contributed to the increasing intellectual preoccupation with the study of nature.

No less effective, however, in the secular direction was what happened in the *strictly religious domain*. The church, in its contest for supremacy over the worldly powers, was bound to become a worldly power itself, deeply involved in political matters and relaxing its spiritual discipline in its preponderant concern with possessions, prestige, and grand ostentation. The corruption, simony, exploitation of the people, the political misuse and mass-use of spiritual penalties like excommunication and interdict, are too wellknown to be detailed here. As a result, the official church with its secular clergy was undermined from within and from without, by the monastic as well as by the heretic movements.

Monasticism itself, intended as a spiritual corrective to

106

ecclesiastical degeneration into this-worldliness, succumbed time and again to a similar laxity, all the more so since the orders were put to use by papal policies; and ever new waves of reform—from that of Benedictus of Aniane in the ninth, the Cluniacensians and Camaldulians in the tenth, the Cartusians and Cistercians in the eleventh and twelfth centuries, up to the foundation of the mendicant orders in the thirteenth century—had to bring back to the mind and the conduct of life the intrinsic aims of Christianity. Between monastic reform movements and heretic movements cross-influences and interactions occurred, and the border lines between them were often fluid. Heretic groups, like the Cathari (Bogomiles and Albigenses) were residues of ancient sects which in apocalyptic and patristic times had somehow been related to Christianism, and Manichaean dualism persisted in the very doctrine of Christianity, in the division of angels and devils, heaven and hell, spirit and body. The Waldensian *pauperes* and the Franciscan *spirituales (fraticelli)* were one in their emphasis on the original Christian virtue of poverty, and were both hunted down by the Inquisition.

At the end of the twelfth century the church still exercised prodigious authority over the common people. It seemed to confirm and fulfill the double role with which Augustine had invested it: With its resplendent organization, its crusading appeal, its feudal overlordship of rulers, such as the kings of Sicily, Aragon, and England, it appeared indeed as the earthly surrogate and precursor of the Kingdom of God, gradually uniting all nations into a *universa gens,* a universal community. At the same time, the church dispensed, in its sacramental capacity, anticipatory salvation to the individual soul. But underneath this resplendent appearance, incited by the unscrupulous conduct of the clergy, a movement emerged, which proved of great reformatory consequence, and of particular importance regarding the evolution of the concept of history: The road to salvation which Augustine had raised to a wholly spiritual sphere, was brought back to earth, where it had been in the times of Israel; it was continued and re-historicized under the aspect of the new, medieval situation.

A new concept took shape simultaneously and, as far as we know, independently, in France and in Italy at the end of the twelfth century: In Paris the cleric and schoolman Amaury *(Amalricus)* of Bène (died 1204 or 1207), and in Italy the Cistercian abbot Joachim of Flores (died 1202), both expected the great turn of times to occur in their near future and arrived at similar notions of a gradual progression of salvation, temporalizing the Holy Trinity into three evolutionary stages or *status:* a first period, the age of the Father, from the Creation to the appearance of Christ, a second period, the age of the Son, starting with Christ's Passion and continuing until their own time, and a third period, expected to set in presently, and lasting to the end of times: the period of the Holy Ghost.

Amaury of Bène was the more immediately revolutionary of the two, but less penetrating and influential in regard to the dynamization of the static medieval views of man's relation to the Absolute. His heretical notions are based on a radical, ultramystical pantheism which bridges early Areopagitic Neoplatonism and the later mysticism of Master Eckhart. Besides, Platonic and Aristotelian elements, which stirred the minds of the twelfth century, mingle in his theory; and the tenets ensuing from this whole mixture are extreme. His fundamental thesis is: Whatever exists is God; God is everything and all: God is the form, essence, and existence of all things. He is always, in all time, hence he is in time, and time is in him. Accordingly, he is also now, in this moment. God is omnipresent, therefore he is everyplace. Since God is everything and works everything in everybody, he effects the good as well as the evil. Consequently, he who has recognized God as the maker of everything in him is incapable of sinning, and if somebody attributes what he is doing to himself and not wholly to God, he is in a state of ignorance which is hell. Hell is nothing other than ignorance, and paradise is nothing but the knowledge of truth.

From these views it necessarily follows that sacraments are useless and transsubstantiation illusory. Faith being identical with knowledge, the emphasis shifts to spirit, and the rule of the Holy Ghost is believed to be ultimately incarnate in every human being. Just as the Law of the Old Testament, incarnate in Abraham and the patriarchs, had been supplanted by the apostolic teachings, incarnate in Jesus Christ, so in the same way the Law of the Gospels was to be supplanted by the guidance of the Holy Ghost, incarnate in the *"spirituales"* of the final stage of humanity.[1]

Joachim of Flores, a less eccentric Christian and more momentous thinker, arrived at a thorough, explicit, and detailed historization of the road to salvation. It was no longer, as with Augustine, a communal or personal process of transcendence, but, similar to the original Jewish conception, a concrete advance *(ascensio)* toward perfection here below: salvation will not come "at the end of times," but in time itself.[2]

[1] Cf. G. C. Capelle, *Amaury de Bène* (Paris: Bibliothèque Thomiste, 1932), particularly the *Textes* 3, pp. 90 ff.
[2] Cf. Herbert Grundmann, *Studien über Joachim von Flores* (Leipzig-Berlin, 1927); Ernesto Buonaiuti, *Gioacchino da Fiore* (Roma, 1931); Ernst Benz, *Ecclesia Spiritualis,* (Stuttgart, 1934); Herbert Grundmann, *Neue Forschungen über Joachim von Fiore* (Marburg, 1950).

Joachim's thought is, however, more elaborate and methodical than was the guiding idea of the Old Testament. Of necessity, it takes in all that had happened and had been debated in the meantime; a new, more articulate consciousness had developed. Joachim proceeds from a close connection, indeed unity, of the Old and the New Testament, which to him seems to document a coherent process of human transformation, transformation of the individual mind, and transformation of the communal order: *"Life must transform because the condition of the world necessarily transforms"* and "the Holy Ghost must change our mind . . . to the effect that in a certain way we are not what we were, but begin to be different."[3]

The transformation of the mind *(spiritualis intelligentia)* does not occur, as with the mystics, as a purely personal, immediate illumination which could happen at any time and in any period, but in a common evolutional advance from the knowledge of the course of things human *(scientia)* to a limited insight into the divine background of human existence *(sapientia ex parte),* and finally to the fulness of spiritual cognition *(plenitudo intellectus).* This mental evolution corresponds to a transformation of the human community from a sensuously palpable to a wholly spiritualized status. In the first stage, the age of the *Father* (and the married men), we were subject to the Law, therefore were in fear and servitude; in the second stage, the age of the *Son* (and the clerics), we were subject to grace, therefore given to faith, but still in servitude to the sons, i.e. the church. In these two periods the aims of salvation were still conveyed to men in tangible, but enigmatic signs, symbols *(figurae),* and sacraments. But the divine truth is revealed gradually in such

[3] Quoted by Ernst Benz, *op. cit.,* p. 26. (Italics mine.)

110

a way that in each transition the sacraments of the higher *status* imply the culmination and abolition of the sacraments of the lower *status*. In the third *status,* the stage of the *Holy Ghost* (and the monks), all men will be free in a realm of spirit and love. This will mean a detachment from sacraments altogether, due to the fullness of spiritual illumination, and, accordingly, the deliverance from the rule of the church. It will be an age of *monastic community,* a community of humility, poverty, and love.

This whole concept constitutes a historization of divine revelation, correlative with the transformation of humanity. It is a realization of the spirit in both senses of the word: the externalization of the divine spirit coincides with the internalization of mental grasp, with the innermost human cognition of the divine. By his method of "typological exegesis" (the demonstration of the concordance, *concordia,* of *signs* in the previous stages with the progressively *realized events* in the later stages) Joachim sees the supersession of the Catholic Church by the ultimate spiritual community as analogous to birth, death, and resurrection: just as David succeeded Saul, and John the Evangelist succeeded Peter, so the order of spiritual men will succeed the bishops; just as Peter, according to Jesus' prediction, died as a martyr and was survived by John, so the Papal Church will die and be survived and superseded by the "Spiritual Church." The whole divine and human career of Jesus Christ is seen as an individual prefiguration of the destiny of the church: What Christ had undergone in his suffering, death, and resurrection, happens on a sublimated level to his mystical body corporate, the church. The "Spiritual Church" has been hidden in the Catholic Church, and with its realization in the end-state, in which the evangelical commands of poverty and humility will appear in full purity, a state that was always expected as the Kingdom of God will have arrived.

According to this general tendency toward a sublimated *communization of the personal destiny of Jesus Christ,* the figure of the Messiah assumes a somewhat indistinct, inconclusive character. In conformity with Joachim's whole concept, the actual leader into the realm of the Holy Ghost was supposed to be the monastic order *(ordo spiritualis)* itself, the vanguard of the ultimate transformation of humanity. Joachim, however, seems to have been unable clearly to educe the last consequence, and dispense completely with a personal leader, whom he vaguely characterized as a kind of "angelic pope," a "bringer of the gift of the Holy Ghost" and transformer of the Catholic Church into a "Spiritual Church," a "new leader" assembling the perfect and righteous.

Joachim pointed to the evangelical community of the twelve apostles as a prototype of his spiritual community, and he even spoke of a return to that original Christian form of life *(redire at formam illam),* but only "in analogy"—*the fulfillment lying in the future, not in the past.* The original evangelical form of life was shown only as an exemplary simile of and point of departure for the future realization, the *evangelium aeternum.*

But there is another feature of this historization of the road to salvation which displays some affinity to the original Jewish notion. The Augustinian passive submission to predestined grace is abandoned. Evangelical life is not a mere sign of divine election, nor is it a hidden life in transcendent eternity, it is an active anticipatory contribution to a future historical realization. The sacrament does not in and of itself save and protect a person; it does so only if the recipient by

112

his conduct of life *(moribus)* makes real what the sacrament only signifies. In the formative stage, therefore, the life of the Christian will be a *vita activa,* and only in the last period "the practice of *vita activa* (but also the need of sacraments) will vanish, and the fruit of a *vita contemplativa* will ripen." The time of struggle, as formerly signified in the reign of David, will end, and the time of peace, previously hinted at by the reign of Solomon, will arise.

Historization has a further important consequence. What to Paul and to Augustine was the faithfuls' "hidden life above" is transformed into the life of a generation of the future, a vanguard generation which in the period of transition is contemporaneous with the still dominant generation of the previous stage. These vanguard members of a spiritualized community are precisely those called on to bring about the age of the Holy Ghost. Here, Joachim raises the problem of overlapping generations which in our twentieth century has become a much discussed issue of historiography, particularly art history.[4]

It is evident how Joachim's views conflicted with the doctrine and the claims of the official Catholic Church, and how they were bound to undermine its authority. All the many variances derive from Joachim's historization of the Trinity, the revelation, and the process of salvation. The dynamization, temporalization of the Trinity into stages *(status)* could be construed as a division of its unity. All the claims of the church rested on the assumption of a single, past revelation, which was to be valid once and for all, on its "catholicity," on its earthly substitution of the Kingdom of God and, implicitly, its sacramental mediation—there-

[4] Cf. Wilhelm Pinder, *Das Problem der Generation* (Berlin, 1926–1949).

113

fore, the uninterruptible succession of the popes, the "vicars of Christ" until the end of time. The Papal Church considered itself a mystical embodiment or rather reincorporation of the incarnate Son of God, a *"corpus mysticum Christi,"* in which all human stations were divine "vocations" and therefore stable and inalterable. All these claims were challenged by Joachim's concept of transformation.

This concept may be seen as an expression, in religious guise, of a new historical consciousness, indeed as a theological prefiguration of the Hegelian self-realization of the absolute spirit and its manifestation in a collective order; in simpler terms, Joachim's monastic community corresponds to Hegel's ideal state. Even the dialectical manner of this process is rudimentarily foreshadowed. Joachim rather than Augustine may be regarded as the ancestor of the philosophy of history.

10

THE IDEAS OF JOACHIM AND HIS PRECEPT OF A COM-
munal life of evangelical poverty, humility, and spirituality
lived on in the new mendicant orders of the thirteenth century, most particularly in the Franciscans. And after this
order too, very soon, inclined to laxity and was put into the
service of the papacy, an intransigent minority among them,
the *spirituales* or *fraticelli,* persisted in following the evangelical teachings of Joachim, preaching and glorifying the
evangelium aeternum, until in the fourteenth century they
were, as a heretical sect, handed over to the Inquisition.
Indeed, their influence reached the political sphere in the
fight of the emperor Louis IV (Louis of Bavaria) against
the Avignon pope John XXII, and the concomitant grotesque controversy about the poverty of Jesus Christ. Even
the revolutionary legislation of the Roman "tribune" Cola
di Rienzi, who, in 1347, ruled the city for half a year,
showed traces of Joachimite inspiration.

Still more consequential than the influence of Joachim's
evangelical message was the impact of his prediction that
the turning of the times was near: during the whole thir-

teenth century people felt close to the age of the gospels; they believed that the blessed era to come would be of a kind with original Christianity.[1]

It was truly an epochal turn. The Hohenstaufen Emperor Frederick II (1194–1250) assumed his revolutionary rulership (1215)—the apotheosis of the Middle Ages and the inauguration of the Renaissance. An evangelical world was expected, but a fundamentally Antichristian, thoroughly secular one, emerged. The epochal turn came with the struggle between Frederick and his powerful opponents, the popes Gregory IX and Innocent IV, which climaxed the age-old rivalry between the imperial and the papal dominion; but it was strikingly manifest in the ambivalent attitudes and ambiguous career of Frederick II himself, now crusading, now banned by the pope; rising along with the ascendance of Franciscan evangelism whose "John the Baptist" Joachim had been; taking advantage of the anticlerical and apocalyptic temper of the epoch and likening himself to Augustus, ruler of the golden age of peace, the age in which Christ was born, but ultimately, when he claimed even the spiritual leadership of Christianity, to Jesus Christ himself. He was hailed as the prince of peace, the Messiah and Supreme Judge of men, and cursed, not only by the papal Guelfs, but also, prominently, by the Joachimites, as the devil prince, the Antichrist, who from evangelical times was expected to precede the advent of the millennium, deceptively resembling the Messiah. Ever again, through the centuries, the Antichrist had been announced by Sibylline prophecies and seen incarnate in various heathen rulers, Nero, Domitian, Mohammed. But never had any figure come so his-

[1] Ernst H. Kantorowicz, *Frederick the Second,* new ed. (New York, 1957), p. 335.

116

torically close to the image of the Antichrist as, in the twilight of the thirteenth century, this Christian emperor, breaking through the bounds of Christian institutions and claims with the ruthless, blasphemic tyranny of his last years. This was the actual *historization of the Antichrist,* followed not by the Kingdom of God, nor by the reign of the Holy Ghost, but by the consummate emancipation of man.[2]

[2] Cf. Ernst H. Kantorowicz, *op. cit.,* Chapter IX, pp. 603 ff.; Ernst Bernheim, *Mittelalterliche Zeitanschauungen in ihrem Einfluss auf Politik und Geschichtschreibung,* Part I (Tübingen, 1918), pp. 97 ff.; Franz Kampers, *Die deutsche Kaiseridee in Prophetie und Sage* (München, 1896), pp. 69 ff.

11

WE HAVE FOLLOWED THREE MAIN EVOLUTIONAL
lines leading to secularization and historization, the *scholastic*, the *religious*, the *political*, all of them, in fact, *still dominated by the religious concern*—i.e. man's relation to the absolute—all of them interacting and converging. But there is another, equally important line, which we have to trace briefly, that is, *the course of daily life itself*, in which of necessity the secular concerns prevail. From the twelfth century on, the cities began to rise and consolidate as a result of the expansion of trade, which in turn was a consequence of the reopening of the Mediterranean through the Crusades and the Christian reconquests of Southern Italy, Sicily, and the greater part of the Iberian peninsula. The crowding of urban life and its commerce demanded increasing organization and particularly a more methodical and flexible administration of justice, which meant systematized law and revival of jurisprudence. In the tumultuous early centuries of the Middle Ages legal procedures had been based on diverse, irregular, and cumbersome customs of barbarian tribes, on local traditions, and on social depend-

encies of various kinds. General legislative directions in secular affairs could only be derived from Roman law, which, to be sure, in Rome itself, being its local tradition, had survived in a fragmented and popularized practice. But practice in this casual, unprincipled form could not have effected that vast concentrating power which Roman law exerted in the later European centuries, when it helped cement whole nations and states. What was needed was systematic jurisprudence, the study and understanding of the Roman codes, the most important among these being the *Digest,* a summary of the writings of the great Roman jurists, which reappeared in the eleventh and twelfth centuries.

The *revival of Roman law,* its study and teaching, was initiated around 1100 by the celebrated jurist Irnerius at the University of Bologna. He separated the study of law from rhetoric, one of the traditional liberal arts, and thereby established jurisprudence as an independent discipline. In his *Glosses,* he analyzed and interpreted complicated passages of the *Corpus,* literally, and with reference to other pertinent parts of the texts, and instructed his disciples by means of questions and discussions. He fathered a whole school, indeed generations, of *Glossators* who added their commentaries to those of their predecessors and, somewhat comparably to the Talmudic Gemara and Halacha, entwined the texts with their proliferating glosses which often swelled to whole volumes.

This intellectual activity of the Glossators had far-reaching consequences in various directions. Their training of the mind in subtle distinctions, which even in their Roman ancestors had been exalted as "written reason," not only developed jurisprudence into a "rival, . . . a secular rival" of theology, as Haskins remarked, it influenced scholastic

119

speculation and "performed a pioneer task of dialectical analysis peculiarly suited to a logical age working on a rigidly limited body of material."[1] It achieved this by "a disposition to push a principle to its extreme logical consequences, and an equally strong disposition to harmonize it at all costs with a seemingly contradictory principle; a passion for classification, for definition and minute distinction, a genius for subtlety . . ."[2]

From the University of Bologna the study of Roman law spread to other universities, it passed into practice and it began to exert its regulative influence not only on municipal life, but on the political scene all over Europe. Canon law, in many respects a filiation of Roman law despite its religious substance, was codified around 1140 by Gratian, a monk from Bologna. This *Decretum Gratiani,* a "Concord of Discordant Canons," bears the traces of the school of Irnerius and, being the first authoritative textbook of canon law, loosed it from theology proper. From then on, all conflicting political interests began to avail themselves of legal arguments for their support.

By far the most trenchant effect of this reactivation of Roman law was the aid it afforded the secular princes in their attempts to subdue their feudal lords and round out their territorial powers into national states. Roman law was the mighty instrument to be used against feudal law and municipal freedoms. The emperor Frederick Barbarossa was one of the first to refer to it, with the assistance of the Bolognese jurists, in his claim of supremacy over the Lombard cities. Gradually, the "legists" were drawn into the

[1] Charles H. Haskins, *The Renaissance of the Twelfth Century* (Cambridge, Mass.: 1927; New York: Meridian Books), Chap. VII.

[2] H. Rashdall, *The Universities of Europe in the Middle Ages* (Oxford, 1896), quoted by Haskins, *op. cit.,* Chap. VII.

permanent service of princes and monarchs, and finally became their most loyal ministers, helping them to establish their absolutistic regimes and administrative bureaucracies. By this means, one could say, Roman law had a decisive part in the formation of the European nations and of the political structure of a secularized world.[3]

The legal consolidation of purely secular dominions carried far beyond its practical ends: By transforming theological and metaphysical concepts into political abstractions, it started a movement which, passing through the phase of the dynastic nation-state, ended up in the establishment of fullgrown nations, which embrace the whole populace and involve its uncancellable presence, active or passive, in government. Thus, the new legal order tied down and stabilized earthly life and afforded it an autonomous substance and permanence. In short, it brought about a *real and complete secularization of time,* which, theoretically prepared as it was by Augustine, had never yet taken practical effect. This process was greatly furthered by a notion emerging at that time in close connection with the consolidation of the territorial states: the doctrine of *perpetua necessitas,* that is, of a continuity of practical needs inherent in the continuity of political life and institutions, indeed in the natural persistence of things.[4]

While in the domain of scholastic thought, it was the victorious nominalist trend which, through rationalism and science, paved the way to secularization, the jurists achieved the same result by exploiting the realist point of view. Platonic, Neoplatonic, and Aristotelian influences had, each

[3] Cf. Franklin J. Pegues, *The Lawyers of the Last Capetians* (Princeton, 1962).
[4] Cf. Ernst H. Kantorowicz, *The King's Two Bodies* (Princeton, 1957), pp. 284 ff.

121

along its own lines, brought scholastic metaphysical thinking to equate the Christian angels with celestial intelligences, emanations of the divine spirit, divine forms and prototypes, and finally, genera and species.[5] Ernst Kantorowicz, in his study *The King's Two Bodies,* which is in fact a history of the genesis of political abstraction, has demonstrated how these transformations of scholastic realism came to be successfully used by the jurists for the stabilization of political regimes.

We recall that the problem of the nature of time was one of the crucial queries which had plagued Augustine and had given rise to the distinction between three temporal modes: eternity *(aeternitas),* i.e. divine timelessness, time *(tempus),* the limited stretch of the humans and the world here below from creation to an unpredictable advent of the heavenly Kingdom, and, in between the two, the aeon *(aevum),* the sphere of the angels, who also were created by God, but immortal. Later, the Averroists introduced Aristotle's embarrassing view of the infinity of time proper, in which, to be sure, creation and destruction of all things cyclically recur. Both, the infinity of time and the recurrence of all events, were unacceptable to any Christian view: neither the principle of divine creation, hence the beginning of human time, nor the uniqueness of the human progress toward salvation could be sacrificed. "The world," says *Kantorowicz,* ". . . did not turn 'Averroist' as a result of the teaching of a Siger of Brabant . . . and other masters in the faculty of arts at the University of Paris: the world

[5] Thomas Aquinas identifies the angels with wholly incorporeal, spiritual substances connected with bodies only in their capacity of "impellents": every angel represents a species. Cf. Ueberweg-Baumgartner, *Grundriss der Geschichte der Philosophie der patristischen und scholastischen Zeit* (Berlin, 1915), p. 498.

remained Christian. Nevertheless, what had been epidemic in the thirteenth century, became endemic in the fourteenth and fifteenth: one did not accept the infinite continuity of a 'World without End,' but accepted a quasi-infinite continuity; and one did not believe in the uncreativeness of the world and its endlessness, but one began to act as though it were endless; one presupposed continuities where continuity had been neither noticed nor visualized before; and one was ready to modify, revise, and repress, though not to abandon, the traditional feelings about limitations in Time and about the transitoriness of human institutions and actions."[6]

Now the *aevum* was the time of the angels—who were considered to be *created*, spiritual beings, but endowed with immortality—and the angels came to be likened to the "collective abstractions," or "immortal and immutable species."[7] In this way the jurists undertook to safeguard the supra-individual perpetuity of dynasties, regimes, and the state. The concept of perpetuity extended to the people,[8] with reference to the old Roman *lex regia* which had it that all imperial power be conferred by the people. It lived on in the assumption of the immortality of nations.

Mortal individuals were thus distinguished from the indestructible continuity of the royal dignity, of the Crown, of the "body politic" or "mystical body"—the secular de-

[6] Kantorowicz, *op. cit.*, p. 283.

[7] The angels, originating in the retinue of the Persian Ahura Mazda, later the Biblical messengers of God, underwent curious transformations. Plato replaced the mythical deities by Ideas, divine in their own right. The Alexandrians Philo and Clement, the first Jewish, the second a Gnostic Christian, identified the Ideas with the angels. In scholasticism they returned to their significance of "celestial intelligences," and in this roundabout way ended up being equated by the jurists with their "immortal and immutable species."

[8] Kantorowicz, *op. cit.*, p. 301.

scendant of the *Corpus mysticum Christi.*[9] The King was immortalized by the distinction of "two bodies" of the royal person, the "body natural" of the individual and the "body politic" of his legal status, which in England was explicitly characterized as a "corporation sole."[10] (Likewise, the church, in order to protect her prestige, separated the fallible person of its priests from his consecrated officiation.)

All such legal concepts, however, growing out of a quasi-independent development, which started with the revival of jurisprudence around 1100 and the recovery of the *Digest,* converged with another quasi-independent development gradually legitimizing a trend which pervaded all political life from the twelfth century on. I have mentioned the rise of the cities as a result of the new flourishing of commerce, and their need of a reliable common law. But it was also a period of transition, in which feudal lords gave way to territorial princes. Rulers of a new kind began to prevail, taking advantage of the decline of the overstrained imperial power by assembling in their hands all the diverse rights, prerogatives, offices, and properties in a territory and uniting them into an autonomous dominion. More and more the administration of these dominions required stabilizing regulations and bureaucracies which later transformed estates into states.

In the course of the consolidation of dynastic dominions, all sorts of *political practices,* which had been occasioned by recurrent exigencies, grew into steady routine and, finally, ended up as permanent legal institutions. Kantorowicz quotes various examples of such perpetuations: the emer-

[9] Kantorowicz, *op. cit.,* pp. 15 ff.
[10] The French version of such abstraction was: "Henry, Charles, Louis meurent, mais le roi ne meurt pas. (Henry, Charles, Louis die, but the King does not die.)"

124

gence of an "impersonal fisc 'which never dies,'" the conversion of feudal *ad hoc* dues into regular public taxation (this too had its parallel and example in the papal perpetuation of crusade contributions into continual indulgences and fixed church levies); the development of extraordinary envoys, delegated for special negotiations, into regular, legally trained *procuratores*, and finally permanent embassies and "foreign services"; and so forth.[11]

[11] Kantorowicz, *op. cit.*, pp. 284 ff.

12

THE OUTCOME OF THE VARIOUS CONVERGING AND IN-
terconnected movements which we have seen, all of them
tending to shift the point of gravity from supranatural to
mundane life, was, to put it briefly, the *secularization of
immortality*. The genera and species being immortal, "time
now became the symbol of the eternal continuity and immortality of the great collective called the human race, of
the species of man, of the seminal powers, of the forces of
germination," and "the unlimited continuity of the human
race . . . made meaningful . . . the craving after worldly
fame, the *perpetuandi nominis desiderium,* which increasingly became a decisive impulse for human actions. . . .
Fame, after all, made sense only in this world and if mankind were believed to be, in one way or another, permanent
and immortal; and if Time was Life, and not Death." " 'Immortal fame' in this world" may be considered "as the
equivalent of or secular substitute for the immortal beatitude
of the other world. . . ."[1]

[1] Ernst H. Kantorowicz, *The King's Two Bodies* (Princeton, 1957),
pp. 277 ff.

In antiquity, great conquerors and rulers wished to be connected with the divine, either through descent from or identification with a god or mythical hero, or through personal deification. Alexander traced himself from Achilles and from Jupiter Ammon; Pompei, in his triumph, wore a robe supposed to have been Alexander's, and inscribed his feats on a temple built for Minerva from his booty; Augustus wanted to be a second Romulus, as Diocletian a second Augustus. Eminent men looked backwards for the commemoration and eternization of their names. Now, with the incipient Renaissance, a new look, a *forward look* was born. People wished to appear, and be remembered, in their own name, in their unique, singular selfness, they wanted to become immortal in their capacity as mortals.

Finally, the new look, the forward look, announced itself in a first, rudimentary awareness of *secular progress*. Even at the beginning of the Christian era, under the regime of Augustus, material progress had been noted, but it had been seen as a sign and preparation of the advent of the millennium. It was part of the Christian progress toward salvation. But the new notion of Progress, noticeable first in the twelfth century, was no longer connected with the religious process. It was based on the observation of a general advance of human knowledge, it was the result of an expanding consciousness. This first notion of purely secular progress, to be sure, did not yet reach into an unlimited future, it was still restricted by the persisting terminus of the "end of times." It is, however, worth registering as a symptom of the mounting weight of earthly experience.

In the so crucial twelfth century, we find such recognition of mental advance attested by various authors. They all derive their reflections from a casual remark of the Roman grammarian Priscian (sixth century A.D.), whose work, The *Institutiones grammaticae* seem to have been widely used in the twelfth-century teaching of the liberal arts. With reference to other authors in his field, Priscian had observed that "the younger they were, the more perspicacious" *(quanto juniores, tanto perspicatiores)*. This dictum, which apparently had been passed over without special notice by previous generations, was now taken out of its special context and gave rise to momentous general inferences.

The earliest known scholar to take notice of Priscian's sentence, seems to have been Bernhard, a master of the School of Chartres at the beginning of the twelfth century. He was credited by his pupil John of Salisbury with saying that "we are like dwarfs sitting on the shoulders of giants so that we can see more and farther than they have seen, not because our eyes are any sharper or more acute, or bcause we are bigger than they were, but because we are lifted up and carried on high by the gigantic magnitude [of the past]."[2]

Somewhat later, in the middle of the century, the German bishop, Otto of Freising, a learned Cistercian, and a military leader in the Second Crusade, wrote a chronicle, entitled *Historia de duabus civitatibus,* "A History concerning the two Cities" (i.e. the City of God and the City of Man), starting, in the Augustinian vein, with Adam, but leading up to his own time of the Hohenstaufen Empire. In the prologue of the fifth book, again referring to Priscian's

[2] *"Dicebat Bernardus Carnotensis nos esse quasi nanos gigantium humeris insidentes, ut possimus plura eis et remotiora videre, non utique proprii visus acumine aut eminencia corporis, sed quia in altum subvehimur et extollimur magnitudine gigantea."* Quoted by George Sarton, "Standing on the Shoulders of Giants," Query No. 53, *Isis,* XXIV (1935–1936), I, pp. 107 ff.

remark, which, he says, belongs to "the first things school-boys used to hear," he writes: *"The more advanced the age in which we are placed, the more maturely are we instructed by the progression of time and the experiences of things.* By understanding the things invented by our predecessors in the same spirit as they did, we are able to invent new things. Hence many things which were concealed from our predecessors, men of radiant wisdom and eminent ingenuity, were revealed to us by the process of time and the course of events. So, regarding the Roman Empire, which because of its excellence was considered eternal by the pagans, and almost sacred by our Christians, what became of it, everybody can see."[3]

But the most advanced notion of Progress, we find expressed around 1200 by the Bolognese jurist Azo, a disciple of Irnerius. His theory reaches well into the modern age, indeed it anticipates the dominant tenet of the eighteenth and nineteenth centuries. In the prologue to his *Summa Codicis* he maintains that human nature is apt to be constantly improved through knowledge and an ingrained habit of study: "Since after the invention of knowledge *(Scientiae)* . . . [man's] acuteness of mind was endowed with successively new gifts of nature, it is not surprising that *by continuous exercise the human condition receives some increment.* . . .Custom itself is turned into nature, wherefore those being younger visualize more perspicaciously the individual

[3] *"Hinc est, quod multae antecessores nostros, preclarae sapientiae ac excellentium ingeniorum viros, latuerunt causae, quae nobis processu temporum ac eventu rerum patere ceperunt. Proinde Romanum imperium, quod pro sui excellentia a paganis aeternum, a nostris pene divum putabatur, iam ad quid devenerit, ab omnibus videtur."* Ottonis Episcopi Frisingensis Chronica sive Historia de duabus Civitatibus, second edition (Hanover and Leipzig: Scriptores Rerum Germanicarum, 1912), p. 226. (Italics in the text my own.)

things." Knowledge itself may become a permanent characteristic of human nature. "Because the ancient masters of arts and science have carried together the principles, they are praiseworthy; but," Azo concludes, "they should not be extolled above all others, since he that subtly emends a fact should be lauded more than he that first invented it."[4]

We see here—in the successive views of three men of the twelfth century—the development, step by step, of a historical consciousness, for the first time *universal, unique, and secular*. Polybius, as we have noted, had become aware of a tendency toward progressive enlargement of the scope of historical units. But what he was able to visualize as the climax and end-result of this trend was the Roman Empire, a still particular political body, not the all-encompassing coherence of the human race and of human nature. Besides, his view was still bound by the pattern of eternal recurrence. Judaeo-Christian thinking saw man's progress toward salvation as a universal and unique happening, but it was dominated by a hieratically stable absolute, and its progress was directed toward a fixed end. Only the sharp Pauline and Augustinian severance of spirit and body, and the ensuing release of purely secular interests and activities made possible the kind of historical consciousness which we find evolving in men of the twelfth century.

Bernhard of Chartres gave prominence to Priscian's casual remark and generalized it by applying it to all scholarship. He still recognized the superiority of the ancients and attributed the greater perspicacity of his contemporaries to the "gigantic magnitude" of the knowledge assembled by

[4] I owe the information about the theory of Azo and the above quotations to Ernst H. Kantorowicz, who generously permitted me to use the manuscript of a planned study on the Idea of Progress in the Middle Ages. (Italics mine.)

those who came before them. *Otto of Freising* arrived at an awareness of the fact that the advance of the human age and the mere accumulation of recorded events, the "process of time" and "the experience of things," carry our mental vision farther and higher than that of former generations. He exemplifies it by contrasting the grand illusions of the ancient Romans, pagan and Christian, about their empire with the later evidence of its transience. He even stresses the recent ability, based on prior achievements, to "invent new things": Man became the maker of things, and it was worth his while to make them. Finally, *Azo's* theory that custom, by making characteristics constant, brings a species closer to perfection, and that in this way the human characteristic of learning, by becoming customary, is capable of bettering human nature, verges on the modern idea of Progress. For him, as Kantorowicz comments, "progress has its immanent goal, which is permanent."

We are at the threshold of the modern age in which human history comes to enter upon its very own, independent, purely secular course.

13

THE RENAISSANCE MARKED THE BEGINNING OF MAN'S settling down on earth for good. Undermined by scholastic analysis, as well as by mystical heresies which went over into the successive reform movements, the degenerated church split; its true catholicity ended and it shrank to a party, theological and political. True, the transition, like all transitions, was slow, and the contest between the forces of Reformation and Counter Reformation remained a prominent issue in the sixteenth and seventeenth centuries. But, symptomatically, the Thirty Years' War, which had started as a religious conflagration, gradually turned into hegemonial conflicts, and religion dwindled in public life into a less and less relevant, sanctimonious superstructure of sheer power struggles.

For a time the rivalries of dynasties occupied the public scene; underneath it all, however, intellectual controversies went on between conceptual exponents of national attitudes, such as French rationalism versus British empiricism and naturalism. Science gained the upper hand over the philosophical speculation from which it had sprung. Again, as in the Middle Ages, conceptual movements, which were themselves given impetus by the course of events and experiences, had, in turn, very real and actual effects.

Toward the end of the eighteenth century, there occurred an over-all shift of conditions, more radical even than that of the Renaissance; although apparently abrupt, it had been long in preparation.

The growing weariness with rational discipline, the malaise, the "failure of nerve"—to use Gilbert Murray's phrase—of the aristocracy, and, on the other hand, the spread of Enlightenment, its marriage of rationalism and empiricism in the sciences, commingled with the accumulated popular discontent to erupt in the French Revolution. This revolution, together with the British Industrial Revolution —on its part a result of scientific and technological advances and the economic rise of the middle class—recast much more than the actual life of the people: a momentous change took place in the relation between actuality and conceptuality, a change that deeply affected the constitution of human consciousness. The basis of political and economic happening broadened, *happenings were socialized,* as it were; and, similarly, *philosophies were socialized into ideologies,* that is, into secular doctrines—capitalist, socialist, racist—which gathered under their banners not only schools, but ever larger, ever more ingrained, "indoctrinated" popular groups. While science, as actualized in technology, began to permeate daily life on all levels, thereby intellectualizing it; and while all techniques and operations grew more and more rational, ideologies, for all their surface rationality, turned more and more irrational. As a consequence, the interaction of concept and performance, theory and praxis, which formerly was readily distinguishable, had now become most complex and intricate.

So, as seen from the present climax of these developments, the vicissitudes of political history, i.e. the power struggles between dynasties and nations, with all their diplomatic and military ramifications, which have been, and still are, treated as *the* substance of history proper, reveal themselves to be transitory events. They appear as a transition from a spiritually to an ideologically and scientifically dominated age of man; and on another level they seem to have served as the limited instruments of a secular transformation, namely, of the *consistent broadening of historical units*[1] *and the expanding scope of consciousness that went with it*. In themselves they have come to assume for us a secondary importance; they are relevant only as exponents of a deeper, underlying process of history.[2]

Viewed from the vantage point of the resultant situation in which we find ourselves today, the history of the modern age appears to be basically the history of diverse parting, ramifying, and specializing human functions, among which

[1] The secular evolution proceeds from tribal units to cities and city-states—even the Roman Empire is still a city-state, as are the Renaissance city-republics—from city-states and feudal principalities to territorial estates and states, from national monarchies to real, popular nations, finally from ideological power blocs to the technically prepared potentiality of an organized "one world."

[2] To be sure, nationalism has today, and will have for a long time, a tenacious afterlife, obsolete as it essentially is. People, enmeshed in the turmoil of present-day foreground events, fail to distinguish ideological from national concerns and invest ingrained ideological attitudes with a national nimbus. Newly liberated peoples pass through a stage of ardent national self-assertion. But, in contrast with former national liberations, as for instance the independence movements of the Netherlands and of America, the present liberation from colonialism is at the same time a social liberation, and the new nations, try as they may to steer a purely national course, have great trouble, in this tightly interconnected world of ours, to avoid being drawn into the mesh of the dominant ideological struggle.

the *complex of economy, science, and technology has come to predominate and determine the course of events,* actual and conceptual. Today, we witness the final stage of the long process of growing together, of increasing interaction and interpenetration, almost to a point of unity, of the three, from their beginnings somehow connected, fields of activity: science, technology, and economy. Militant by way of ideologies, these three have also seized and almost completely integrated in their complex the military function and apparatus of doctrinal power blocs.

The thorough secularization of human life from the Renaissance on has involved a dimensional change in the relation of man to his world. The ancient and medieval cosmos which had comprised the human together with the extra-and suprahuman world, is sundered, and the pious study of a divine order of cosmic forms and elements has given way to the purely rational study of purely material nature. The basic relation of human faith and divine grace has been displaced by the relation of man's rational capacity to an infinitely explorable and exploitable opposite material, the relation of subject to object. The one feature that this new relation retained from the previous one was the belief in the absolute stability of nature, a vestige of the divine absolute.

This change implied a shift in purpose, specifically the growing prevalence of purely functional purpose, in the study of man's environment. To be sure, all human activity, and so all study, originally sprang from some purpose. But in antiquity, as mentioned before, as well as still predominantly in the Middle Ages, man wanted primarily to find out how to conduct his life in the right manner, that is in accord

135

with the divine and cosmic order. It is equally true that the practical pursuit of functional purposes, i.e. occasional observation and invention, started with the beginnings of man. But only now, in the new, secularized world do we find purely functional purposes methodically pursued to the growing exclusion of the broadly human ones.

This phenomenon is intrinsically connected with the methods of *abstraction,* which originally trace back to the theory of Aristotle. But it is Thomas Aquinas, a confirmed Aristotelian, who has provided the classical formulation of the process of abstraction and who, by this formulation, which involves the concept of the "law of nature," has laid the foundation of modern science. The premise is the assumption that only individual entities, issuing from the conjunction of spiritual form and potential matter, possess independent reality, and that "our cognition of individual things precedes our cognition of generalities *(cognitio singularium est prior quoad nos quam cognitio universalium)."* The general, immanent in individual things, "is released through abstraction from individual matter *(universale fit per abstractionem a materia individuali),"* and in this way true knowledge is attained, for "true knowledge is concerned with the general *(scientia est universalium),"* that is, with the essence *(quidditas)* contained in individual things, the common forms and features, the species *(formae exemplares)* and the causes of things *(rationes rerum).* But, from this extraction of general species, features, and causes out of individual entities, Thomas distinguishes still another mode of abstraction, namely the singling out of something, for reasons of convenience and simplification, while disregarding everything else *(abstractio per modum simplicitatis).* The process and progress of modern science is based on the

136

combination of these two kinds of abstraction. It starts from "the cognition of individual entities," i.e. empirical observation, and proceeds through the establishment of common "laws of nature," and increasing isolation of specialized complexes from luxuriantly multiplying factual material.

The abstraction of "laws of nature" presupposes the distillation of immutable common features and causes from a variety of individual entities and processes. This involves *classification* and *quantification:* to find out what is common to a variety of things, or beings, one has to distinguish their species and features, in other words, *classify* these species and features. This, in turn, implies quantification. The unique individual in its integral wholeness is incomparable, its unique processes are irreversible and unrepeatable. To classify species and features, one has to abstract them from the unique individual entities, make them comparable and repeatable, and this again means making them spatially and temporally "commensurate," as precisely definable—i.e. limitable, measurable—as possible. The almost self-perpetuating concentration and time-contraction of abstraction led inevitably to the mathematical means of communication which has become the over-all language of science. Finally, the codes of cybernetics have driven the function of abstraction to a point where it has become amenable to out-and-out automatization, i.e. to the transfer to machines, and by this palpable medium abstraction to the nth power expanded into the actuality of daily life.

These methods of equalization and reduction, applied to the variety of individual entities, were correlated with *analysis,* that is, dissection of individual entities, a procedure which ramified and grew ever more subtle in connection with the process of scientific abstraction. Scientification,

137

combining abstraction and analysis, spread not only to the scholarly studies dealing with human affairs, but through its application—technology—it extended to human life itself. Automation is but a symptom of a general process which pervades our world: the accelerating conquest of nature by a science which passes immediately into technology, and is, in turn, pushed along and sustained by technology. More and more, the human being is acting through machines, living by and among machines; in the conduct of his life he is reduced to directing from an ever more remote place an ever more complex and overwhelming apparatus. Observing the rapid increase of population, we may foresee the gradual vanishing of nature, landscape swallowed up by buildscape. Natural growth is displaced by artificial *making,* a process which is very near to reaching life itself. All this reacts on the human being. In his very making, man is circumscribed by the application of his applied scientific laws and by the systems and machineries it produces. Mechanization attacks human spontaneity, the creative growth in man himself.

Along with this weight of science and technology, interconnected and converging with it, went what I called the "socialization of happenings," the merging of discreet happenings into a continuous flow of developments. The overpowering pressure of the masses called for organization and formal regularization of government, for statistical quantification of man's every move. I need not dwell on the more obvious results which I have dealt with in another context:[3] the dwindling of individuality through over-all collectivization, standardization, and functionalization of human beings.

There are other effects of this whole historical trend, the

[3] Erich Kahler, *The Tower and the Abyss* (New York, 1957), Chap. II, III.

crucial one being the *transformation of consciousness*. The ever narrowing specialization (abstraction *"per modum simplicitatis"*) of daily proliferating sciences and technological innovations, together with the endless accumulation of global events, which keep multiplying through people's immediate reactions to the immediate reporting of events, produced an enormous and constantly swelling material which no individual mind can contain. All this material, being registered and stored by some specialized institution, scholarly, publicistic, or political, is sectionally known and evaluated, though in no way correlated and integrated by a coherent mental control. The ever changing body of this accumulating knowledge amounts to a *collective consciousness*, a diffuse, impersonal consciousness, as it were. To the degree that this impersonal, collective consciousness grows, the personal consciousness of the individual shrinks, overwhelmed by the unending onrush of impenetrably complex "knowns." Under the pressure of such demands the perceptive capacity of the individual gives out, he is prone to retreat into his parochial privacy, and, if forced to a public move, to resort to doctrinal or emotional shortcuts, that is, to the drives of his unconscious.

So we have arrived at a stage, in which the hypertrophy of an uncontrolled collective consciousness corresponds to the atrophy and loss of control of individual consciousness, a situation that results in the *gradual ascendance of the unconscious*. Consciousness is the medium of thinking and reasoning, of seeking coherence of some kind, it is the condition in which the human being, on the basis of his feeling of identity and orientation in his world, is able to draw conclusions as to how to conduct his affairs to propitious and productive ends. The transformation of consciousness, therefore, involves a *transformation of reason,* or, more particularly, a *split between reason and its offspring, rationality.* Reason is a human faculty, inherent in the human being as such, rationality is a technical function, a technicalization and functionalization of the ways in which reason proceeds. Functionalization makes rationality capable of being detached from its human source, and generalized as an abstract, logical method. Again, this process ultimately goes back to Aristotle's *Organon,* particularly his *Analytics.* But it is only rather recently, in consequence of the general process of specialization, and of the ensuing transformation of consciousness, that rationality has become completely independent of, indeed radically opposed to human reason. And just as the expansion of collective consciousness entails the shrinking of individual consciousness, rationality grows at the expense of reason.

To give just one, the most salient, example of this development: A scientist, or engineer, working on the problems of nuclear weaponry and warfare is, in his special research, compelled to proceed with the strictest rationality. As a private person, however, he may well succumb to all kinds of emotional bias, professional or ideological indoctrination, or just the functional enthusiasm for his work. As far as human reason comes in at all, it is effective only in the narrowest personal scope of concern for keeping his job and pursuing his career, and even the care for the destiny of his children is repressed and held back from any connection with the dire implications of his work. To ponder over the general human consequences of his activity hardly occurs to him; indeed, according to the scientific canon of strict confinement to a delimited field of research, such inferences are considered to exceed his competence. A scientist demonstrating that, given certain protective measures, a nuclear war will cost the nation only fifty, instead of hundred and fifty million human beings, and therefore is "feasible," such a man, when confronted with the problem of human values, will reply, with the pride of his compartmental amorality, and a-humanity, that these questions are none of his business, and that his concern is strictly with well-defined technical problems. In the field of medicine for instance, rationality works toward the most subtle means of therapy and medication. Years may be devoted to saving the life of a single child, while, in the field of war technology, rationality juggles the lives of millions of human beings as mere proportional figures. The most dainty comforts are produced alongside of colossal destructivity. The prevalence of reason in human affairs would presuppose a comprehensive evaluation of all factors, including psychic and generally human factors, in a given situation. But in the anarchical condition of an incoherent collective consciousness, functional rationality has reached a point of autonomy where it simultaneously serves the most contradictory ends, among them purposes which human reason must regard as monstrous insanity.

So the state at which developments since the beginning of the nineteenth century have arrived, is characterized by a coexistence of overrationalization and irrationality, and indeed as far as the complex of science, economy, and technology is concerned, by divergent overrationalization *producing* irrationality. In the arts, we notice a similar divergence of trends. Art, in the modern age, assumed the heritage of religion, inasmuch as it carried over into secular life the manifestation of cosmic wholeness. Artistic form appeared to be the last, intrinsic, residue of the otherwise

141

dissolving absolute. There are recent performances in music, painting, poetry, however, which show a definite tendency toward the deliberate breaking up of form, and a branching off into opposite directions: scientistic, mathematical, indeed mechanistic, construction, and its overcompensation, boundless release of the unconscious, and, through the free association of the performing act, a search for lost personal identity.

The dominant feature of the modern age is the triumph of rationality. The achievements of science and technology are formidable and imposingly evident to everyone. Much less recognized, however, is the danger inherent in this boundless expanse, unchecked by any countervailing effort. We might have learned from the experiences of the last fifty years how an overrational civilization can collapse into the worst—because mechanized—savagery. We witness today the emergence of sheer irrationality, the loss of reason, from panlogicity. Rational methods have immensely extended the reach of our vision, intrinsically as well as extrinsically. But something essential has escaped this supposedly ever progressing rational "control of nature." In the progress of this "control of nature" we have lost control of ourselves, of human nature and the human world. Science recognizes the infinity of its task, it has long since settled into its sheer movement. It has even begun to discover that the ground, on which it moves, is itself moving. But it seems to be not sufficiently aware of the fact, that by rationally extending its grip on our world, it has changed this world and its inhabitants with it. This is where nature escapes, and will always escape: by its dynamism, by its protean mystery, which is the only thing that really persists.

14

A̲T THE BEGINNING OF THE MODERN AGE, THE EXPE-
rience of scientific discoveries, technological inventions, and
geographical explorations strengthened and broadened the
belief in secular Progress. The three basic innovations, decisive in establishing this secular tenet, and constantly referred
to in the modern centuries, were the mariner's compass, gun-
powder, and the printing press; the first advanced navigation, and thereby overseas exploration and commerce; the
second revolutionized the methods of warfare, and by this
means uprooted the feudal system; and the third introduced
the quick dissemination of news, knowledge, and doctrinal
propaganda (Luther's success was largely due to his pam-
phlets). No less important, but less emphasized, probably
because of its dangerous implications for the dogma, was
the telescope, invented in Holland and perfected by Galileo
and Kepler, which made possible the verification and completion of the anti-Ptolemaean and anti-dogmatic Copernican system, with all its far-reaching consequences.

The idea of secular Progress, in making its headway, had
to overcome two powerful traditional forces, Christian or-

143

thodoxy and Renaissance classicism. (Occasionally, it was helped by their mutual opposition, Machiavelli for instance maintaining the Renaissance attitude as against the Christian, and later, conversely, Desmarets de Saint-Sorlin extolling the gains of the Christian age over antiquity.) Actually, however, the idea of Progress carried over into its secular faith the Christian doctrine of man's road to salvation.

We have seen how even in the Middle Ages, under the dominance of a still-unshaken Christian belief, the concept of secular Progress had already taken shape. As a secular enclave within the Christian time-span the care for secular progress had developed. The expectation of the "end of times" was not abolished, it just grew dimmer, and was gradually ignored, it faded into oblivion. Otto of Freising had considered his time, the twelfth century, the *senium mundi,* the old age of the world, simply because of its wealth of knowledge, referring to the prophecy of Daniel: *"plurimi pertransibunt et multiplex erit scientia* (many will have passed, and knowledge shall be plentiful)." But this observation had been connected with a sharp awareness of the limits set by the Second Coming.

Some four hundred years later, Francis Bacon, whose main concern was already the progress of knowledge, still intimated such an unpredictable end, just by stating that the world in which he lived has entered its old age. But he went a step further and raised a crucial point, relevant even today. He explicitly reversed the order of ages: In point of fact, he says, the "ancients" are the youth of the world *(Antiquitas seculi juventus mundi),* and the modern are the old. And as it is rightly assumed that old people, with their accumulated knowledge and experience are wiser than youth, so the same may be taken to hold for the modern age, and ever accruing

144

knowledge can be expected from it: ". . . to circle the earth, as the heavenly bodies do, [Bacon still refused to accept the heliocentric system] was not done nor enterprised till these later times: and therefore these times may justly bear in their word . . . *plus ultra* in precedence of the ancient *non ultra* . . . And this proficience in navigation and discoveries may plant also an expectation of the further proficience and augmentation of all sciences because it may seem that they are ordained by God to be coevals, that is, to meet in one age . . . as if the openness and through-passage of the world and the increase of knowledge were appointed to be in the same ages . . ."[1] And, extending Bacon's views, an English clergyman, Joseph Glanvill, in his book *Plus ultra, or the Progress and Advancement of Knowledge since the Days of Aristotle,* (1668) arrived at an attitude which is very common in our days: We have more reason, he says, to be grateful to the unknown inventor of the mariner's compass "than to a thousand Alexanders and Caesars, or to ten times the number of Aristotles."

At the beginning and for quite a time afterwards—from Bodin, Bacon, Descartes to Pascal, Charles Perrault, Newton and the Abbé de Saint-Pierre, the belief in Progress followed that old argument *quanto juniores, tanto perspicaciores,* whereby the *juniores* were now regarded as the *seniores.* This argument implied that progress consisted purely in technological and scientific discoveries, that is, inventions, observations, experiences. All these innovations were based on the assumption of the absolute stability and immutability of nature, and so also of human nature. What was supposed to progress were only the new findings and

[1] *Novum Organum,* 129; quoted by J. B. Bury, *The Idea of Progress* (New York, 1932), p. 55.

uses. On this basic assumption of an absolutely stable nature the striving for strictly causative connection, quantification, and mechanization of nature proceeded—at first still unsystematized and mixed with astrology and Neo-Pythagorean symbolism—to the search for a reliable *"ars inveniendi,"* art of invention, and to projects for cooperation and association of inventors, all of which involved studies concerning a fundamental *method* of research and cognition. Finally, Descartes laid the groundwork for both, epistemology, and the concept of invariable "laws of nature," thereby completing the break with the Christian tradition: his thorough mechanization of nature was, as demonstrated by Malebranche, incompatible with Divine Providence. (Considering the present state of knowledge, it is interesting to note, that in the course of the controversy between the *Ancients et Modernes,* when Perrault and Saint-Sorlin concluded from the permanence of vigor in lions and trees the permanence of the intellectual capacity of man, Fontenelle argued in reverse that without the premise of the stability of nature science would be impossible.) Descartes's call for a "universal science" found its fulfillment in the "solidarity of sciences," as manifested by the Encyclopedists, and in the foundation of the Royal Society and the various European academies.

The movement toward an accomplished doctrine of Progress was not rectilinear—as in fact no developments are—it periodically regressed under the doubt and scepticism of even those who ultimately, under the sway of rationalism, promoted it. So, a classical scholar, Louis Le Roy, in his book *De la vicissitude ou variété des choses en l'univers* (1577; second ed., 1584) draws attention to the ruin of many great accomplishments of previous civilizations and weighs the idea that the same destiny may be in store for those of his own age. Divine Providence, he believes, distributes equally and justly good and evils among the various peoples at their appointed time so that every one of them may enjoy an epoch of excellence in special fields of activity, yet may be prevented from overbearing. So far, this appears as a peculiar circular theory, the concept of a *circle through circulation of excellence*. In the end, however, Le Roy envisions a definite progress of the modern age, referring not only to the perfect novelty of the three basic inventions but—in a prophetic, though still utopian statement —to the fact "that the whole world is now known, and all the races of men; they can interchange all their commodities and mutually supply their needs, as inhabitants of the same city or world-state."[2] We have here the first combination of a circular with a progressive concept, followed by the very similar theory of *"circular progress"* of the British divine George Hakewill in 1627, by Vico's much broader *Scienza nuova*, 1725, and, in our days, by the theory of Toynbee. Common to all of them is a still predominantly theological point of view. On secular grounds Voltaire's sardonic critique and Rousseau's civilizational scepticism were the most influential reactive agents in the development of the belief in Progress. Both men, however, not only ended up in programs or ideas of educational and democratic reform, but their very criticism of Progress stirred and sustained the movement.

So in tides of argument and counterargument the conviction prevailed that the moderns were certainly equal, and in some respects (knowledge and its applications, and even the arts) definitely superior to the ancients. Actual events

[2] Quoted by Bury, *op. cit.*, p. 45.

broadened concepts, just as broadened concepts promoted actual events: not only technology and transoceanic discoveries, but also the consolidation of national states, the splendor and glory of the regime of Louis XIV, the colonial and economic expansion of the Netherlands and England, and the commercial and financial innovations it entailed, and finally the successes of the Dutch, the English, the American revolutions.

Gradually—and this was an advance most effective in the American and French revolutions—the theory of Progress was extended from the restricted field of human capacities, which thrived on the accumulation of knowledge, to the broadly social and moral condition of man. This meant an *activation* of the concept. Progress of knowledge and technical praxis was no longer merely propounded, it was to be systematically used for the material well-being and the moral advancement of humanity. To be sure, human nature was still considered fundamentally stable, yet nonetheless improvable through enlightenment and amelioration of external conditions. Azo, in the twelfth century, had assumed that "custom turning into nature, knowledge itself may become a permanent characteristic of human nature." And now people had arrived at an awareness that knowledge, ever broader knowledge, in leading to the betterment of living conditions, would make human beings themselves not only happier, but better. Therefore, the Encyclopedists aimed most particularly at the promulgation of knowledge.

This assumption implied, conversely, that whatever was bad in human conditions and in the nature of the human being was due to ignorance and superstition, to wrong institutions and states of affairs. So through Descartes's "universal reason," deified in the French Revolution, and in its application to social and political institutions, *man* was seen to be *perfectible;* a belief which reaches from the Abbé de Saint-Pierre and Fontenelle in the seventeenth century to Hegel and Karl Marx in the nineteenth. In fact, with Fontenelle and Montesquieu the doctrine of Progress was almost complete. Man, according to Fontenelle, will never age, nor intellectually degenerate, but, on the contrary, ever improve through further knowledge. Progress is certain and infinite, it has its necessary order and sequence, it is autonomous and impersonal, that is, independent of the persons who serve it: if Descartes had not existed, Progress would have used another man. Similarly, Montesquieu excludes Fortune as well as Providence as agents in history. "It is not Fortune," he writes, "that governs the world . . . There exist general causes *(causes générales),* moral or physical, which are at work in every monarchy, raise it, sustain it, or bring it down. Every thing that happens is subordinate to these causes. And should any given battle, that is, a particular cause, undermine a state, then there existed a general cause which made that state liable to perish by a single battle. In short, the main current of events *(l'allure principale)* sweeps along all single events."[3]

At this point where not only man's ability to experience, to gain knowledge and to invent, but his whole social and moral being is considered perfectible, perfectible by the very means of his faculties, a new state of consciousness is achieved. It is at this point that the secularization of the religious concept of salvation is completed. Salvation becomes *the self-salvation of man.*

This came to pass in *three general stages* (not strictly chronological, but evolutional, i.e. as gradual shifts of em-

[3] *Grandeur et décadence des Romains* (1734), Chap. XVIII.

phasis). *First,* the accumulation of secular experiences had led people to realize that in knowledge itself and the application of knowledge men did progress: "By understanding the things invented by our predecessors in the same spirit as they did, we are able to invent new things." Here, in Otto of Freising, and even much later still, in the age of Louis XIV, the *present*—the human age reached at the time—was seen as the peak of human progress. (For Perrault the glories of Louis and Corneille represented the summit of all time.) Man was so impressed with his secular development up to this point that he did not look any farther, particularly since beyond this secular present the divine beyond still loomed powerfully.

The *second* step is Francis Bacon's who, undisturbed by the thought of an "end of times," looked *beyond his present,* *"plus ultra,"* inferred future progress from past progress, and made plans for it. The *"plus ultra,"* however, was for him and his follower Glanvill, still indistinct.

The *third* stage was reached by the men of the Enlightenment and the French revolutionists, pre-eminently Condorcet and Cabanis, who expected a *realm of human perfection,* the "indissoluble union" of liberty, equality, virtue, and matured intellect, to materialize as the final result of the revolution. Indeed all ideological revolutionaries since then —so also the Marxists, aiming at their "classless society" in which politics and war were to disappear—have been inspired by this prospect.

The fixed goal of perfection, toward which Progress was expected to move, was conspicuously stressed by the German philosophers of the Enlightenment and of romanticism. Kant's *Idee zu einer allgemeinen Geschichte in Weltbürgerlicher Absicht* (Idea of a Universal History from a Cosmopolitan Point of View, 1784) leads up to this final goal by what I would consider the most neatly consistent, indeed the most radical presentation of the arguments of the Enlightenment. He includes in it a more carefully reasoned version of what before him Émeric Cruce, Louis Le Roy, and the Abbé de Saint-Pierre had envisioned, and which in our present predicament is our only hope: a supranational world organization.

In this concept Nature has clearly and explicitly assumed the role of God—more radically and explicitly even than in the formulations of Diderot and Buffon. Nature, in the form of universal Reason, guides the destinies of the world and of man with wilful and providential determination. And human will and reason is used by her as an instrument of her own will and reason. In this way natural determination and human will coincide: "Nature has willed that man shall produce wholly out of himself all that goes beyond the mechanical structure and arrangement of his animal existence, and that he shall participate in no other happiness or perfection but what he has procured for himself, apart from instinct, by his own reason . . . As she gave man reason, and freedom of will on the basis of reason, this was at once a clear indication of her purpose in respect of his endowments . . . The invention of his own covering and shelter from the elements, and the means of providing for his external security and defence . . . as well as all the sources of delight which could make life agreeable, his very insight and prudence, and even the goodness of his will, all these were to be entirely his own work. Nature seems to have taken pleasure in exercising her utmost parsimony in this case and to have measured her animal equipments very sparingly. She seems to have exactly fitted them to the most necessitous requirements of the mere beginning of an existence, as if it had been her will that man, when he had at last struggled up from the greatest crudeness of life to the highest capability and to internal perfection in his habit of thought, and thereby also . . . to happiness, should claim the merit of it as all his own and owe it only to himself . . ."[4]

Kant drives this theology of Nature and Reason so far as to paraphrase the story of Genesis, by assuming that for this purpose man, in order to develop his rational and moral qualities to self-perfection, had to pass through a patently criminal (sc. sinful) state; otherwise, "men might have led an Arcadian shepherd's life in complete harmony, contentment and mutual love" (sc. in paradise), "but in that case all their talents would have forever remained hidden in their germ. As gentle as the sheep they tended, such men would hardly have won for their existence a higher worth than belonged to their domesticated cattle . . . Thanks be then to Nature for this unsociableness, for this envious jealousy and vanity, for this unsatiable desire of possession, or even for power! Without them all the excellent capacities implanted in mankind by Nature, would slumber eternally undeveloped. Man wishes concord; but Nature knows better what is good for his species, and she will have discord. He wishes to live comfortably and pleasantly; but Nature wills that, turning from idleness and inactive contentment, he shall throw himself into toil and suffering (sc. 'in the sweat of thy face shalt thou eat bread') even in order to find out remedies against them, and to extricate his life prudently from them again."[5] This argument, being an answer to, and

---

[4] Immanuel Kant, *Principles of Politics*, ed. and trans. by W. Hastie (Edinburgh, 1891), pp. 1–29, Third Proposition.

[5] Kant, *ibid.*, Fourth Proposition.

integration of, Rousseau's theory of man's "Fall" into the evils of civilization, had been used before by Turgot and hinted at later by Hegel.[6]

So the final goal which rational Nature appears to have intended for man, but which only the latest generations will be lucky enough to enjoy,[7] is "the advance out of the lawless state of savages and the entering into a Federation of Nations. It is thus brought about that every state, including even the smallest, may rely for safety and its rights, not on its own power or its own judgment of right, but only on this great international federation *(Foedus Amphictyonum)*, on its combined power, and on the decision of the common will according to laws ... All wars are ... so many attempts —not, indeed in the intention of men, but yet according to the purpose of Nature—to bring about new relations between the nations; and by destruction or at least dismemberment of them all, to form new political corporations ... till at last, partly by the best possible arrangement of the civil constitution within, and partly by common convention and legislation without, a condition will be attained, which, in the likeness of a civil commonwealth and after the manner of an automaton, will be able to preserve itself."[8]

Kant's concluding projection of the course and end of Progress constitutes the germ of Hegel's elaborate scheme of the self-objectivation of "Universal Reason" *(Weltgeist)* materializing in an ideal state: "The history of the human

[6] Hegel, *Logic*, trans. by William Wallace (Oxford, 1874), Chap. II, pp. 46 ff.

[7] ". . . that it is to the happy fate of only the latest generations to dwell in the building upon which the long series of their forefathers have laboured, without so much as intending it and yet with no possibility of participating in the happiness which they are preparing." Kant, *op. cit.*, Third Proposition.

[8] Kant, *op. cit.*, Seventh Proposition.

race, viewed as a whole, may be regarded as the realisation of a hidden plan of Nature to bring about a political constitution, internally, and for this purpose, also externally perfect, as the only state in which all the capacities implanted by her in mankind can be fully developed."[9]

With Hegel and Marx, who were the last to set a definite goal of human perfection without looking beyond this ideal end-state, as if in it human life would settle down in lasting bliss, the notion of the self-salvation of man, and even more, the whole age-old dream of a final salvation came to an end. Instead, actually, humanity had to settle down in a state of lasting provisionality, of endless approximation to a never realizable, ever receding perfection. Fontenelle had already observed: *"Il est évident que tout cela n'a point de fin* (it is evident that all that has no end)." Human affairs spread out in all dimensions, as a consequence of the very expansion of knowledge and analysis. Science, technology, industry, world commerce, extended the outlook; psychology and art deepened it. And a further developed historical consciousness began to reveal reality as a constant, interminate flux.

[9] Kant, *op. cit.*, Eighth Proposition.

15

A<small>LL</small> THESE DEVELOPMENTS WERE THE END-EFFECTS of long preparations. The Aristotelian conception of the *infinity* of time had crept in, as we have seen, hardly noticed in the pursuits of secular life. Its open recognition was delayed by the rule of the dogma. Even the word "infinity" was dreaded, and, in the sphere of physical nature, was replaced by limiting expressions: *minima* and *maxima*. But not only did *Giordano Bruno*—who was burned at the stake —openly expound, in succession to Copernicus, the *extensive* infinity of the universe and its sidereal bodies, but by his *minima* he precluded the notion of an *intensive* infinity: "Space is infinite," in the words of Hermann Weyl, "not only in the sense that it never comes to an end; but at every place it is, so to speak, inwardly infinite, inasmuch as a point can only be fixed step-by-step by a process of subdivision which progresses *ad infinitum*."[1] The concern with the continuum, eventually leading up to the creation, by Leibniz and Newton, of differential and integral calculus, developed along-

[1] Hermann Weyl, *Philosophy of Mathematics and Natural Science* (Princeton, 1949), p. 41.

side the realization of secular continuity in the consolidation of states and institutions. In all these various aspects *secular infinity* was recognized.

Another innovation was the experience of *secular universality*, which became manifest first in the thought of *Jean Bodin* (1530–1596). He and his school introduced comparative history and comparative jurisprudence. Medieval glossators had confined themselves to the study of the Roman *Corpus Juris* and an internal comparison of related passages. Bodin reached beyond the parochial emulation of antiquity, and particularly the pedantic observance of everything Roman, which had come to a climax in the Renaissance. His very heeding of the humanist ideals of classical erudition and clarity led him to a more thorough study and critique of the ancient sources. The result was not only a correction of medieval interpretations, and an inclusion of additional legal material which he discovered in ancient Rome so as to integrate the whole extant body of Roman law into a unified system, but an extension of this system by comparison with, and incorporation of, the legal principles of other states. "The divergencies in history . . . or the laws peculiar to one state or another, are systematically classified in order to compare them and select the best. And finally these institutional diversities of peoples are correlated with major differences in their natural environment or political organization in order to discriminate the special factors which must be considered in evaluating laws. With Bodin, accordingly, a transition is finally effected from the exegesis of authority to a method of critical reflection and a general theory of law. And in some respects the natural law systems of the century which follows, as well as the comparative jurisprudence of the eighteenth century, are continuations of his program."[2]

This juristic reform of Bodin is only part of an even more important *historical* universalism. He repudiated the concept of a Golden Age and of human decadence, and saw progress in human knowledge and inventiveness. His real innovations, however, consisted in his forming a first concept of *secular universal history* and of the world as a *"universal state,"* and in his replacing the traditional four monarchies, into which earthly history had been theocratically divided from Daniel up to Melanchthon and Sleidanus —Babylonian-Assyrian, Persian, Hellenistic, and Romano-Germanic—by the geographic, i.e. neatly secular, division into three world periods, in each of which a particular group of peoples were predominant: the Southeastern, the Middle (Mediterranean), and the Northern. This tripartition became from then on the standard sectioning of "World History"— it later passed over into a temporal, and evolutional periodization. The temporal designation is already noticeable in Bacon's division: antiquities, middle part of time, subdivided into the Greek and the Roman, and "modern history," comprising what for us are the Middle Ages up to the rudimentary modern era in which Bacon lived.

The evolutional structuring, an internalizing of the temporal, begins with *Vico* whose theory (1725), however, was still cloaked in theology and embedded in a *"ricorso,"* a cyclic system. He set forth, in rather clumsy manipulation of the welter of detail generated by the nascent specialization of disciplines, an "eternal ideal history" *(Storia ideal*

[2] Julian H. Franklin, *Jean Bodin and the Sixteenth-Century Revolution in the Methodology of Law and History* (New York and London, 1963), pp. 2 ff. For more detail see this very valuable study.

eterna) or "philosophy of tradition" *(Filosofia dell' Autorità),* in which he shows a human progression in three stages: a primitive condition, in which passions dominate savage, unorganized people, a second, "heroic age," characterized by the prevalence of imagination, or "poetic wisdom," and finally the age of civilization in which the faculty of conceptual knowledge is attained. What is remarkably modern is his attempt to approach each period objectively, through its own mode of dealing with the world, refraining from the use of more advanced concepts, in order to achieve a better understanding.

The periodization of *Turgot,* the finance minister of Louis XVI and prerevolutionary reformer (1727–1781), is entirely free of theological purport, and of circularity, but unknowingly in some accordance with Vico's. It is distinguished by far more clarity, sobriety, and factuality; its anticipation of Comte's[3] three stages has been frequently observed. "Before the interrelation of physical effects was known," Turgot writes, "there was nothing more natural than to suppose that they were produced by intelligences, invisible and similar to ourselves . . . anything that happened without human participation had its god, whom fear or hope provided with a cult, and this cult was patterned after the respect people had for men of power; for gods were nothing but human beings more powerful and more or less perfect according to their being the products of an era more or less enlightened about the true perfections of man."[4] This first phase corresponds to Comte's theological stage.[5] "When the philos-

[3] Auguste Comte, *Cours de philosophie positive,* 1830–1842.

[4] Turgot, *Ébauche du Second Discours en Sorbonne sur l'Histoire Universelle,* in *Oeuvres de M. Turgot* (Paris, 1808), II, 294.

[5] Cf. Vico: "The newly discovered foundations of mythology resulting from the newly detected foundations of poetry, have proved that the myths of the gods are stories from the times when men of the most barbarous paganism believed that all things necessary or useful to man-

ophers had recognized the absurdity of these fables, without, however, having acquired a true understanding of natural history, they ventured to explain the causes of phenomena by abstract terms, like 'essences' and 'faculties'; terms which in fact explained nothing and about which people argued as if they had been real beings, new deities replacing the old ones."[6] It is the phase which Comte calls metaphysical. "Only rather late did people, upon observing the mechanical effects which bodies exert on one another, deduce from these mechanics other hypotheses which mathematics could develop and experience could verify. This is why physics ceased to degenerate into bad metaphysics only after long progress in the humanistic disciplines and in chemistry had enriched the knowledge of interrelationships of things, and this is why, communications between the different societies having grown closer, geographical knowledge has been extended, facts have become more certain, and the very praxis of the disciplines has been submitted to the eyes of the philosophers."[7] This is an almost accurate description of Comte's third, "positivistic" stage.

While these theories already reflect the tremendous and ever increasing impact of the methods and applications of the natural sciences, the cumulative results of these methods have still been "submitted to the eyes of the philosophers." The most prominent and influential one, *Hegel,* undertook to mold the whole inventory of the knowledge of his time into a vast systematic construction and to set down the advanced historical consciousness of the age in an explicit "philosophy of history", combining—as he combined

kind are deities . . ." *Principi di Scienza Nuova, Spiegazione della dipintura proposta al frontispizio* . . .

[6] Turgot, *op. cit.,* p. 294.
[7] *Ibid.,* p. 295.

so much of the European tradition—the geographical with the temporal, the civilizational, and the evolutional division of the career of man. In fact, it was no longer humanity at all, which was the center and protagonist of this vast and complex record, it was the secularized Spirit of Christian antiquity, transforming into modern Reason. Thus, he also combined the four-partition with the tripartition. On a more concrete level, he distinguished four periods, identified with locales, in which the main currents moved: the Oriental, the Greek, the Roman, and the Germanic worlds. On this level, there is still talk of peoples and people. On another, abstractly essential level, man is a mere instrument, or vehicle, or receptacle, of the Spirit, i.e. Reason, of the Universe, which progresses in three stages, from the subjective, to the objective, and finally the absolute Spirit, or Reason. In this concept, as logic is undifferentiated from, indeed identical with metaphysics, and systematic distinctions fuse into evolutional ones, the course of the Spirit, or Reason, advances from the subjective, "ordinary," psychological consciousness of the individual to the objective, general, social consciousness of communities, and ultimately to the absolute, philosophical consciousness, self-consciousness *(Selbstbewusstsein)* of Reason as such. What Kant had specified as a distinct term—the "consciousness in general" *(Bewusstsein überhaupt)*—becomes for Hegel an evolutional end-stage.

Hegel's tripartition of historical stages continues in the dialectical triplicity of the historical movement: thesis, antithesis, synthesis—actually introduced by Fichte.

The coincidence of distinctive terms with evolutional stages, and the fluidization of existential levels and faculties into an all-pervasive process meant the beginning of the full dynamization of reality, but at the same time the apotheosis of Progress.

16

HEGEL'S THEORY OF THE DIALECTICAL PROCEEDING of history had been in effect forerun by the dialectical movement of progress itself in the intrinsically related alternation of optimism and pessimism, progress and regress. Recurrent reservations, based on the experience of the downfall of civilizations, only served ultimately to spur the reform projects and the triumphal revolutions. Progressive optimism from Bacon to Perrault and Saint-Pierre was countered by the scepticism of Pierre Bayle, Voltaire, and Rousseau, and most of the more thoughtful progressive minds wavered between faith and doubt. This fluctuation between thesis and antithesis was, however, prevalently surmounted by synthetic concepts like Turgot's and Kant's. Similarly, advancing progressivism, more and more inclined to look ahead to the promising future and to forget about the past —d'Alembert wanted, like the Futurists of the twentieth century, history to be destroyed—paradoxically retroacted into attention to the past, it actually produced *historism*.

Historism sprang from two convergent sources, a scientific and a humanistic one, namely the *biological evolution theory* and the *romantic movement,* chiefly German, each of which, again, was a synthesis of the rationalistic heritage with Rousseauistic and British naturalism.

Evolution theory grew out of the scientific classification of organic genera whose first systematizer was *John Ray,* called "the father of English natural history" (1627–1705). He and his more famous and influential follower, the Swede *Carl von Linné (Linnaeus,* 1707–1778), still assumed that the various botanical and zoological species were immutably established by God's creation. The development from classification (taxonomy) to genetics is exemplary of the general process of flexibilization and fluidization of man's picture of reality, and, reactively, of human reality itself, a process which rapidly gains ground from the end of the eighteenth century on.

The man who broke down the inflexible barriers of classification was *Buffon* (1707–1788), who opposed the pedantic rational definitions and set rules of the learned men, with the counsel of observation and description of protean Nature—what Goethe called "fixating on nature" *(Hinstarren auf die Natur).* For the sake of simplification and equalization, he declared, the learned men apply the same method to the most diverse and inappropriate cases; they dissociate intrinsically coherent nature and let an arbitrarily selected part of a plant appear as a general characteristic of the whole. Through a countless increase of scientific terms, they make scientific language more difficult than science itself. He wanted nature to be approached without the preconception of an accepted system, *presque sans dessein,* and phenomena to be described most accurately, exactly as they are seen *(représenter naivement et nettement les choses).* By the faithful use of descriptive language the order of nature should be retraced, style being the order and the movement of thinking, accordingly the order of depicted nature itself, as it were. In his attempt to picture animals as precisely as possible he actually inaugurated morphology, the study of the forms of organisms. His principle was to search for the *how* rather than for the *why*. He was already aware of the fluid boundaries between the animal and vegetable kingdoms, and from the fact that some organs of living creatures seem to be no longer useful he concluded that times and forms must have changed.[1]

Again, the opposition between Linné and Buffon was synthesized by *Cuvier* (1769–1832) who attempted a systematization of Buffon's freely observed organic phenomena. What developed first was a rationally articulated concept of organicity. Buffon had arrived at the assumption of "inner forms" *(moules intérieurs)*, prototypes after which the various animals are fashioned, in the manner of works of art, and which allow of variations, but not basic changes. Cuvier proceeds to the concept of a strict correlation of organs and functions in an organic form, every animal being a closed system in which all parts are interdependent and contribute in an accurately established relation to a unified performance of the body. No part can change without its changing all others. And not only does an intrinsic relation exist between organs and functions of an organism, but the whole organism is connected with its environment in a rigorously defined relationship. This is his "law of the conditions of existence *(loi des conditions d'existence)*".

Another of Cuvier's important innovations was the in-

[1] His philosophers were Locke and Rousseau. Locke, by his refutation of Descartes's theory of innate ideas and by his seeing the mind as a *tabula rasa*, gaining content only through inscription of experience, accomplished a break with the past comparable in fact to that of Descartes. His influence on the biological discussion was considerable. Rousseau, for his part, seems to have been deeply impressed by Buffon's approach. When he arrived in Paris, it is told, he went to Buffon's house and kissed the threshold in awe.

clusion of palaeontology in his field of consideration, which amounts to a *historization of biological theory*. On the basis of ample material, Cuvier established the fact that fossils (which Linné had still considered minerals, not organisms) stem from periods in which a fauna, entirely different from ours, populated the world, and that life on earth has changed its character a number of times—due to recurrent destructive catastrophes. This discovery actually prepared the ground for a *history of life on earth*. Cuvier even attempted to use fossilized animals for the determination of geological epochs, in other words, a history of the earth. He finally arrived at the conclusion that the different species, successively emerging from the recurrent "revolutions," show steady *progress in organization*. Buffon had dealt with organisms whose absolute stability he never doubted—a residue of the old belief in the immutability of nature.

The theory of recurrent catastrophes, however, somehow reminiscent of the Aristotelian theory of cataclysmic regeneration, prevented Cuvier from conceiving of true genetic evolution. With all his advances, he still did not quite overcome the notion of the constancy of species, although he went as far as to assume a quasi-genetic development *within* species: a species, to him, is the sum total of individuals who descend from each other or from common parents. He definitely rejected any phylogenetical considerations. *Geoffroy Saint-Hilaire* (1772–1844) extended this internal lineage to the relationship of species with each other, by assuming that all animal forms, including the human, have common organs; he applied to the whole animal world and its species the hypothesis of the Swiss naturalist Charles Bonnet (1720–1793) that all forms which an animal goes through in its embryonic stages are basically one and the same and that

164

the varied embryonic stages differ only in the differential growth of organs. Likewise, Geoffroy Saint-Hilaire maintained that the irregular growth of analogous organs produced the variety of the organic world. He held to the constancy of organs, which were supposed to be common to all organisms, and differences among them were regarded as due solely to different arrangements, complications, or modifications of these same organs. Both, Cuvier and Saint-Hilaire, although influenced by Buffon's artistic concept of an organism, saw the organism rationally divided into fixed, immutable organs, which precluded a recognition of the morphological flexibility prerequisite to evolutional flux.

It was *Lamarck* (1744–1829) who first realized both the flexibility and the fluidity of the organic world. For him—in strict parallel to Hegel who worked out the same in the metaphysical domain, but who repudiated all theory of *biological* evolution—the over-all organization of the organic world becomes coincident with its evolution, as do its taxonomic distinctions with the stages of its evolution. The ancestral line of organic forms, as he conceived it, expressed their systematic order. In his view, coherent evolution of forms is brought about by changes in the natural environment to which organic beings adapt themselves. Use or non-use of organs causes changes in characteristics, and the compulsion to adapt arouses in the individuals an effort to evolve, which furthers these changes.

Finally, *Darwin,* influenced by Malthus who, in his population theory, demonstrated that nature is by no means economical, but rather wasteful in its creations, and that every species produces more offspring than is needed for its maintenance, contrived his now prevailing theory of natural selection: The adaptation to the environment occurs

165

through the "survival of the fittest." In any case, whatever the mode of adaptation, a straight line of progressive evolution from amoeba to man has been established.

The companion process in the humanistic domain went on principally in Germany. It was a continuation, in fact a third, and decisive stage of the fight between "Ancients and Moderns." Just as Buffon turned against rational classification, advocating free observation of nature, the German rebels, Hamann and Herder, led the attack of the "Storm and Stress" movement against fixed rules and rational prescriptions dating back to antiquity, and unfettered the expression of inner nature, the drivings and strivings of emotion and genius. They implicitly opened up an immense panorama of vistas which had been restricted by the constraints of rationalism, and the first reaction was an outburst of promiscuous experiences, studies, reflections, and projects, as the writings of the two leaders show.

Hamann (1730–1788)—together with the poet Klopstock—set the mood of the new generations. His style was an overwhelming and overwhelmed medley of scholarship and lyrical enthusiasm. Hardly anyone understood him completely, indeed he himself confessed that after a while he could not understand what he had written and that it caused him "hot and cold flashes *(Angstschweiss und glühend Gesicht)*." He called his writings "a dunghill, which, however, contained the seeds of everything that he had in his mind *(einen Misthaufen, in dem aber der Same von Allem sei, was er im Sinn habe)*." And he had so much in his mind at the same time that, as Lessing declared, his writings read like examination problems for polyhistors. His "seeds," however, are the seeds of the German romantic movement, and it is important to note that here already rational elements, fragments of erudition, and intellectual subtleties, like the principle and practice of irony, mingle with subjective emotion. The whirl of motley stylistic and vital ingredients, the attempt to embrace the whole released diversity of contents, to convey a feeling of the living whole, this is romanticism in the bud.

In *Herder* (1744–1803), Hamann's most influential prophet and disciple, this contracted literary conglomerate is loosened and expanded into fields of activities and concerns, without losing its amorphous character. Indeed, with the amplified material, the overpowering of the mind by the richness of tasks and experiences is even increased.[2] Herder was receptive to all European trends, and the idea of Progress and the goal of an enlightened and humane humanity to which he was wholeheartedly devoted assumed special importance in Germany, which had not achieved a homogeneous nationality, a national society, a national tradi-

[2] "How much remains to be searched out and cleared up! Our epoch grows ripe for it . . . the genesis of Greece—from Egypt or Phoenicia? Of Etruria—out of Egypt, or Phoenicia, or Greece?—And now the genesis of the Northerners, from Asia, or India, or aborigines? And the new Arabs? From Tartary or China! and the characteristics and forms of all these, and then the coming forms of American-African literature, religion, customs, mentality, and laws—What work there is to be done on the human race! the human mind! the culture of the earth! all spheres! times! peoples! forces! . . . Asiatic religion! and chronology . . . and philosophy! Phoenician arithmetic and language and sumptuousness! Northern religion, law, customs, warfare, honor! The papistic era, monks, scholarship, crusaders, pilgrims, knights! Christian and pagan awakening of scholarship! The century of France! English, Dutch, German forms! Chinese, Japanese politics! Theory of Nature of a new world! American customs and so forth—grand theme: the human race will not vanish, until all that has come to pass and been done! Until the spirit of enlightenment has spread over the earth! Universal history of world culture! (*Universalgeschichte der Bildung der Welt!*)" Herder, *Journal meiner Reise im Jahre 1769* (Memoir of my Journey in 1769). In its seminal jumble, this outburst touches upon the studies and problems of two centuries to follow.

167

tion. All this was still a task to be accomplished in the future. So the stress was on the *future,* on *becoming,* on *movement,* on *dynamic process.* And in Herder we can see most clearly how *the forward look engendered the new look backward,* the historical look; how the belief in Progress and the goal of an enlightened humanity motivated and stirred extensive historical and ethnological studies, searches for the origins of language, religions, and arts; how it deepened the perspective on the past, and broadened the scope of the present. The specifically German task of seeking a national perfection in the human perfection gave Herder's manifold endeavors a didactic and activistic touch. This again moved him to study foreign customs and institutions. His divulging of the folklore and poetry of the most diverse and remote peoples, old and new, Oriental and Western, Southern and Nordic, through description and translation, done with a novel empathy, a keen sense of the characteristic and organic, gives him, in proportion to his time, the function of a Toynbee or Malraux in ours.

The same enthusiastically indiscriminate mixing of elements, particularly the blending of intellectual witticism and boiling emotionalism, characterizes the "storm and stress" movement, whose rationalistic ingredients are frequently overlooked, and the more articulate, elaborate mode of expression of German *romanticism.* Its foremost theorist, *Friedrich Schlegel* (1772–1829), calls romanticism "a progressive universal poetry *(eine progressive Universalpoesie):* "Its mission is not only to re-unite all the separate genera of poetry, and to relate poetry with philosophy and rhetoric. Its intention and calling is, now to blend, now to fuse poetry and prose, ingenuity and criticism, artistic and natural [folk] poetry; to make poetry alive and sociable and life poetic, and to permeate the forms of art with solid learning of all kinds . . . enliven them with the fannings of humor. . . . The romantic style of poetry is still in the state of evolving, indeed this is its very nature that it can for ever only evolve and never be completed."[3]

The most appropriate literary forms of German romanticism are the fragment, in which universalistic minds like Novalis and Friedrich Schlegel could, in a loose and experimental manner, connect and contrast the most distant phenomena, and the freely rambling novel, such as Tieck's, Novalis', or Jean Paul's, in which poetic, satirical, and scholarly components could be intertwined at ease. It is worthy of note that in this period the historical novel made its debut.

German romanticism aimed, as Friedrich Schlegel's fragment indicates, not merely at a new artistic style, but at a new, unfettered way of life, at new social mores; its influence radiated into all spheres of life, politics, the sciences, human communication. It was, in fact, the nucleus of a novel, ubiquitous, protean intellectuality. Its vehicle is *irony*, a special, methodical kind of irony constituting a chain reaction, as it were, of self-surmounting.[4] "Irony," Friedrich Schlegel declares, "is the clear consciousness of infinite agility, of inexhaustible chaos. *(Ironie ist klares Bewusstsein der ewigen Agilitat, des unendlich vollen Chaos)*,"[5] it is reflection "raised to an ever higher power *(potenziert)*" and "multiplied, as in an endless series of mirrors *(wie in einer endlosen Reihe von Spiegeln vervielfacht)*."[6]

[3] Friedrich Schlegel, *Prosaische Jugendschriften,* ed. J. Minor (Wien, 1906), Vol. II, *Athenäum-fragment* 116.

[4] Socratic irony is finite, it is a sociable means to discover truth and ignorance, an instrument of *maíōsis,* delivery (of truth). Romantic irony is intellectual dynamism per se, and endlessly self-perpetuating self-transcendence.

[5] *Loc. cit., Ideen* 69.

[6] *Loc. cit., Athenäum-fragment* 116.

The relationship to Fichte's and Hegel's dialectical process is evident: Fichte's fantastically, solipsistically abstract theory is even more dynamical than Hegel's, based as it is on sheer, endless doing and striving. Being, according to Fichte, has sprung from an original doing, from "consciousness thinking itself, positing self"; self-creating as it is, it is synonymous with action. From this primal reflective action there emerges the ego which posits the non-ego, the outer world, as a barrier for the sole purpose of surmounting it. Restlessly, endlessly does it keep setting new barriers to overrun, new tasks to fulfill. This process goes on indefinitely, since it belongs to the nature of "being as action and striving" that it has no end and cannot be satisfied. Fichte's concept is the perfect prototype of the endless, goalless progress that was to ensue.

17

IN BOTH DEVELOPMENTS, THEN, THE BIOLOGICAL AND
the humanistic, we find the fundamental stability of things
gradually dissolving into flux. The result, historism, inten-
sifies and broadens this trend.

By *historism* we may understand the tendency to see and
explain everything historically; to derive, as we have seen
it done by Hegel and Lamarck, classificatory terms and
distinctions from evolutional stages; systematic and historical order coincide. The very experience of evolution brought
this about, the God- or Nature-given constancies being swept
away in the process.

From the rudimental clutter of preromantic and romantic intellectuality and the speculative systems of the romantic philosophies of history the various historiographical
disciplines gradually unfolded: political history parted with
"cultural history"; sociology with economics and economic
history *(Wirtschaftsgeschichte);* geography with ethnology
which, in concurrence with palaeontology, created anthropology; archaeology engendered art history; history of religion led to mythography; philology ramified into etymology,

history of languages, and linguistics; the history of philosophy diverged from the history of literatures and from the history of science and technological achievements, which were slowly getting underway. Science, to be sure, on its part specializing into ever more fields, remained—with the exception of geology and biology, with its related medical sciences—rooted in the assumption of a stable nature. This was due to the enormous distances separating the human observer from the cosmic-astronomical and sub-atomic changes and processes, the colossal dimensional differences between human and cosmic rhythms and latitudes. Only recently have the expansion and amplification of modern astronomy, astro- and nuclear physics, begun to shake even the faith in the stability of cosmic nature.

The nineteenth century was the heyday of historism. Critical scholarship, methodical research, went back to the sources, unearthed and assembled the basic documentary and monumental records. At the suggestion of the Baron vom Stein, the memorable statesman of the German wars of liberation from Napoleon, the *Monumenta Germaniae historica*, a model enterprise of its kind, were founded in 1824 by Georg Heinrich Pertz. It was the period of the great initial surveys which applied conscientious scholarship to a broad view of epochs, peoples, civilizations, and leading figures—a period marked by the names of Niebuhr, Droysen, Ranke, Mommsen and Jacob Burckhardt, of Tocqueville, Taine, Michelet and Fustel de Coulanges, of Macaulay, Bryce and Maitland. And every one of the newly evolving compartmental disciplines had in this century its founding scholars and synthesizers, needless to enumerate. Again, a new perspective into the breadth and depth of human happening, a new dimension of historical consciousness was opened up. It was indeed the *climax of historical conscious-ness,* evoked by, and within the scope of, individual minds; it took hold of and dominated the temper of the century, it was alive in the thoughts and actions of political leaders, as well as in the mood of the public, and, born as it was from the idea of Progress, it now reflexively enhanced the popular force of this idea.

More and more, however, with the conspicuous exception of the Marxist striving for a social millennium, this general belief in Progress relinquished the expectation of a final state of human perfection, indeed the tenet of perfect-ibility itself. Progress was no longer considered to move toward a definite end; it conformed to the scientific notion of perpetual graduality, of infinitely progressive approxima-tion to an unreachable ideal. In short, it came to coincide with its very process, with *becoming as such.*

This renunciation of finality was connected with another, more substantial change.

Liberalism, based as it was on the doctrine of the scien-tifically and technologically supported endless expansion of economic prosperity through competition, was inherently disposed to such a perpetuity of the progressive process. *Liberal economy, i.e. capitalism,* is in fact predicated on perpetual growth, on ceaselessly expansive movement; it is inseparable from movement. But even *Marxist socialism* began to settle in with endless evolution. Although the evo-lutional faction of Marxism was defeated and seems today bankrupt, having lost its socialist substance altogether, we see the evolutional trend taken over by its fraternal enemies. Communism in its present state, without giving up the prin-ciple of revolution in appropriate situations, appears in-creasingly convinced by the experiences after its victories that a final state of felicity will forever be unattainable. This is manifest in the course of Soviet policy, stronger still in the philosophy of Mao Tse-tung.

The turn of conditions, growing toward the end of the nineteenth century, changed—unnoticed by people—the *meaning* of Progress. As a consequence of the socialization, and, accordingly, the "economicalization" of happenings— which itself had been a result of the French and the Industrial revolutions—the notion of Progress reverted to its original connotation, the significance that indeed had engendered it, namely, the tangibly impressive effects of technological and scientific successes. Technological inventions, we will remember, had been the decisive argument for modern superiority over the ancients. In the meantime, as we have seen, the idea of Progress had broadened to imply the betterment, moral and social, of the human being and of humanity as a whole, by means of increased knowledge and technologically improved socio-economic conditions, by what is called "the standard of living." In socialist theory this belief still persists. But even in socialist practice and everyday attitudes, a renewed identification of Progress with the apparently unlimited strides of modern technology and science has gradually come to prevail: in all camps *man is confounded with his functional capacities*. In point of fact, neither the disillusioning horrors of the world wars and of the Nazi and Stalinist regimes, nor the ghastly degenerative advances of military technology were needed to put an end to the humanitarian significance of Progress; the purely functional interpretation of the concept, the withering away of any human implication, was well underway toward the end of the nineteenth century, long before the catastrophic breakdown of human values in the twentieth; it was indeed a contributing factor to this breakdown.

174

The evaporation of the human content in the idea of Progress was intrinsically connected with a hypertrophical *degeneration of historism into historicism,* which set in at the end of the nineteenth century. In the pursuit of methodical research, an overabundance of data was brought to light which of necessity resulted in an ever increasing specialization. In the minds of scholars, the proliferous material began to overgrow the structural lines of historical processes, all the more so because, according to the positivistic rules of scientific empiricism, any fact has the same validity as any other fact. Students in the human domain were entrapped in a vicious circle: Since a priori concepts of a whole phenomenon—be it a process, an epoch, a people, or a personality—were scientifically unacceptable because they cannot be immediately verified, no absolutely reliable criterion was left as to a distinction between essential and non-essential facts. Without such a distinction, however, no picture of a whole can be achieved. Therefore scholars had to choose between being guilty of subjective selectivity—objective as a man may try to be, there will always be "obstinate" facts—or getting lost in the maze of innumerable equally valid facts, a true *democracy of facts.* To be sure, there were at all times superior minds who chose to expose themselves to positivistic ostracism, but a vast majority of others, anxious to prove themselves impeccably scientific, produced indiscriminate and indecisive accumulations of data, dizzingly analyzed, and filled with them libraries and minds. Overwhelmed by the unmasterable multitude of facts and analytical discussions, scholars can be heard complaining that "we know too much."

The result was a growing stagnation of historical conceptuality, and, consequently, of helpful, comprehensive views. The mass of details, and of ever subtler esoteric controversies, encumbered more than aided orientation. This was the Historicism against which Nietzsche sounded his prophetic warnings. From the beginning of the twentieth century, such scholarly lack of direction began to react on the general state of mind. After the First World War had definitely shattered the belief in Progress as regards its human and civilizational values, and indeed the belief in evolution, which was confused with progress, had fallen in disrepute with it, two conceptual substitutes were left: one was *scientism,* the search for "laws of history," in the manner of Spengler, Toynbee, Sorokin, and others. The other, much more powerful and effective, was *ideology,* the blind, self-blinding submission to a rigid secular doctrine. No such overpowering of the minds by deliberately simplifying orthodoxies, such as we witness today on both sides of the fence, would have been possible without the complete loss of historical orientation, and the more or less general repugnance against the responsibilities of historical coherence.

Nationalism, and *racism,* as they became epidemic in the second half of the nineteenth century, may be seen as precursory, rudimentary forms of ideology, influencing and distorting historical views as they do and positing a particular nation, or "race," as the center of the world. They are still powerful enough today, and besides being active in their own right, they have even carried over into the two giant ideologies which dominate our present world, *communism* and *capitalism.*

Intellectually, under the sway of scientism, the general tendency is anti-historical, in the sense of anti-evolutional. At the beginning of this study, I enumerated the manifestations of this trend in various movements of our time. There is a renewed general inclination to classify and typify phenomena, to treat them, in the manner of science, as stable or stably recurrent, in a moment when in fact the stability of the world is at the point of collapse, and systematization appears to be losing ground; when not only biology but astronomy and nuclear physics as well, are revealing the world ever more as basically a process consisting of innumerable sub-processes.

The same anti-historical, or rather a-historical, turn of mind can be observed everywhere in our lives, in the media of mass communication, in the arts. The atomization of life, the turmoil of hourly news and daily novelties, the ever contracting process of time has approached a stage of universal simultaneity, that is, of spatialization. The fading of perspective in modern painting appears like a symbol of the loss of historical perspective in daily existence and in the vital feelings of people. Humanity, in its technically most advanced stage, seems to have returned to a condition somewhat similar to its most primitive state. People skate on the surface of the present, and historical consciousness, alive only in the individual mind, has generally dissolved into the anonymity and impersonality of the collective consciousness of institutions.

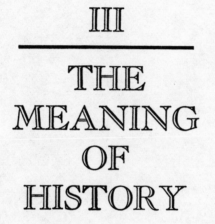

III

THE MEANING OF HISTORY

1

THIS, THEN, ROUGHLY TOLD, AND OMITTING MANIFOLD auxiliaries, is the history of history. In sketching it out, I evidently did not aim at giving a history of historiography, which is quite another matter and should be written quite differently. The premise of this study was that *history is not synonymous with historiography*.

Nor is what I attempted to show solely the history of historical consciousness, which, although it plays a prominent part, is only half of the story. What I intended to demonstrate is the coherent unfolding of interaction between live experience and historical happening on the one hand, and on the other, the accumulation of such experience, i.e. historical awareness; in other words, the indissoluble interaction between actuality and conceptuality. This is precisely what I would call history.

Let me sum up: The innermost problem of the *Greeks* was the experience of *earthly change, in contrast with divine and cosmic permanence.* Their way of relieving this disturbing dichotomy was, first, the conception of the close mythical affinity and constant intercourse between immortal deities and mortal humans. And later, when man came to a clearer awareness of his distinctly human nature and autonomy, and when the conflict between human and divine directions, between immutable substance and variable phenomena accentuated itself more sharply, it was the perennial attempt to reconcile change with the order of permanence, which was the tragic resolution of the Greek existential concern. This conception made for that *incorporation of perpetuity into change itself,* evident in the cyclic view of happenings, the belief in the *eternal recurrence of events,* which pervades Greek thinking from beginning to end. Thus, the Greek world rests on the isomorphism and co-temporality of permanence and circular change. Within this view, however, the interaction of personal experience and concept led to the gradual broadening of historical vision which culminated in Polybius' incipient realization of the convergence of diverse ethnic currents in a unifying superior dominion, Rome.

With the *Jews,* the experience and awareness of *uniqueness,* of the unique destiny of man comes into being. Successive subjugations afford them an immediate experience of the differences among peoples and, by contrast, of a common humanity. The germ of historical consciousness is the sense of the essential identity of man. Their own ever repeated and hence deepened suffering creates in the Jews the desperate yearning for salvation, the notion of their own —and finally all humanity's—movement toward salvation. Here the parallelism between eternity and change is dynamized into a process, a movement toward an end—an end that is the sublimation, through toil and consciousness, of a mythical beginning. And this sublimation through conscious striving makes the process into a *development,* it makes it *unique*. (We remember that even Augustine still sees the difference between the original bliss and the final, completed bliss in the conscious awareness of the blessed condition.) There is, to be sure, as compared with the Greeks, a much greater distance between the Jews and their unique, bodiless, nameless, non-mythological God; and their kind of familiarity with him is very different from that of the Greeks with their humaniform gods. The Lord, the Creator, the Eternal one, personally guiding, commanding, castigating and promising, indeed wilful and jealous, as he manifests himself, is nevertheless pure spirit. On the other hand, however, this spirit is by no means divorced from human life, but rather works with and in it, in its earthly course; the spiritual direction is one with the bodily, the historical road to salvation, and the end, the salvation itself, is an event in which heaven and earth will merge.

Jewish messianic and apocalyptic prophecy, converging with the chiliastic tendencies of all-amalgamating Hellenism, led up to the acts and passion of Jesus. The ensuing deification of Jesus, the *incarnation of God,* as established by Paul, through his use of pagan mystery cults, *reverses the Jewish relationship between God and man.* Instead of the divinely exacted contribution of man to the advent of God's Kingdom, salvation is anticipated by the sacrificial act of God the Son. The general command of God, punishment and reward, are supplanted by the *Grace of God*—a selective Grace, that is—and man's action is reduced to *faith.* Although in this period, the advent of the Kingdom of God, the Second Coming, is still within the reach of expectation, an individual anticipation of eternal bliss is envisioned by Paul in a "hidden life with Christ above" through mortification of the flesh. With the separation of an individual from the general salvation, of a spiritual "life above" from the life of the flesh here below, the ultimate *breach between spirit and body* was introduced. What Paul had started, almost inadvertently, out of the doctrinal, Christological premises, was completed by Augustine in consequence of the world-shaking event, the conquest of Rome by Alaric in 410 A.D. which disproved and confused all Christian prognostications. In order to rescue the Christian community, Augustine, in his *De Civitate Dei,* put off the actual advent of the common millennium into a dim, inconceivable future, and shifted all hope of the faithful to the individual salvation of the predestined elect. Christian life became exclusively a life in the spirit; bodily life was abandoned to its wretched fate. *The radical division of spirit and body is the actual starting-point of secularization.* Deprived of its spiritual sanction, earthly life followed its independent and unholy course. Since life on earth had to go on, the Catholic Church was authorized as a spatially and temporally mediative institution, provisional substitute and lasting preparatory stage of the Kingdom of God, a viceregal power on earth, propagating faith and providing individual bliss. In their ultimate consequence, the Augustinian concepts established the division and power struggle between *imperium* and *sacerdotium,* the militancy of the Crusades and the Inquisition, and finally the imperialistic corruption of the church.

Christianization drew the new Celtic and Germanic forces into the orbit of the Romanized world; the fight against the infidels opened the Christian West to abundant commerce and the influx of non-Christian, pagan, islamic, Jewish, wisdom. Both forces, the Northern and the Southern, intellectually undermined the dogma by logical analysis and by incipient scientific and technological endeavors, a development which finally resulted in the *prevalence of rationalism and empiricism*. The autonomy of reason, as established by the Cartesian revolution, the observation and exploitation of nature, as initiated by the Copernican, Keplerian, Galilean revolutions, secularized the world as much, as did the revival of Roman jurisprudence, which consolidated the territorial powers and nation-states. The Joachimite and Franciscan concepts, actuated by the corruption of the church, fostered heretical and reform movements which eventually split the church.

From the application of scientific concepts the new world power, *technology,* evolved. Encouraged and utilized by enterprising men, from the Portuguese prince Henry the Navigator in the fifteenth century to the British industrialists in the eighteenth, basic inventions gave, in turn, the decisive impulse to the idea of *secular Progress*. In a process of ever closer dialectical chain interaction, the Golden Age, which, in the Jewish-Christian concepts had been held in balance between past and future, was definitely moved from the past to the future, from the norms of the Ancients to the promises of the Moderns. The intellectual movement of progressive enlightenment, the designs of Rousseau, the Encyclopedists and Physiocrats, gave impetus to the *French Revolution,* and with it to the henceforth irrevocable *socialization of events*—the broadening of happenings into processes and of philosophy into ideology—and to the *collectivization of life*.

The Industrial, and that is implicitly the technological, Revolution, brought forth the two ideologies which today dominate the world: The successes of British industry, supported by Whig- and physiocrat-born classical economics and "social Darwinism," produced the doctrine of *capitalism;* Marx, under the impact of the opposite results of the same British industry, namely the condition of its workers, and under the intellectual influence of Ricardo and Hegel, established the doctrine of *communism*. The effects of these clashing ideologies on world events constitute our present predicament.

The notion of Progress reflexly instigated the search for origins, i.e. *historism*. The biological evolution theory and the romantic philosophy of history brought the foundations of reality into flux. The social broadening of events through the French Revolution was supplemented by their temporal deepening through historism and the belief in Progress: both meant the sequential and synchronous fusion of discreet phenomena into processes. The scientific principle of causality did its share: it had sprung from ancient and medieval logic, which was applied to the study of nature, and which was seen as the general mode of natural proceeding. In its extreme form, mechanics, it was established by Descartes and Newton, and advanced by Lamettrie and Holbach. Under the influence of science the search for origins became one with the search for causes. Finally, the advances of modern physics and astronomy completed the recognition of the basic fluidity of all nature.

Technology, exploiting the mechanics in nature, has made tremendous strides since the nineteenth century. The result has been an increasing scientification and mechanization of life, and implicitly its growing rationalization and intellectualization. As a consequence, the relation of actuality and conceptuality has become so permanent and close-knit that the interaction between them which we have surveyed up to this point is now scarcely discernible. "Philosophies," general concepts, are discredited, ruled out as idle speculations, and devoid of influence on actual events; they are replaced by the ceaseless and thousandfold scientific analysis and predictive exploitation of collectivized happenings. If it could be said that in former periods concepts were uppermost in the interrelation between conceptuality and actuality, the reverse appears to be true today: thinking is rather the reflection and projective utilization of actual processes.

2

So HISTORY, IN ITS ESSENCE, IS NEITHER THE GROWTH of historical consciousness, nor the bare course of happenings. It is the interaction of both, and the history of history is the record of this expanding interaction which in its entirety is inherent in our present existence, whether registered consciously or sunk into the unconscious.

Recent theorizers on history often fail to state precisely what they understand by history, nor do they make a clear distinction between the study and the substance of history. Either they identify history with historiography, or, in speaking of history, they vacillate between the act of recording and the material recorded.

However, historians and philosophers seem to agree by now that *history* is *not a science* and has nothing to do with science, the most common argument (first put forth by the German philosopher Heinrich Rickert) being that science is concerned with the general, history with the individual and particular. Reference is made to the vast multitude and abundant variety of singular phenomena—peoples, personalities, happenings, conditions—which are the substratum of history, and which scientific treatment is unable to comprise under general laws. Karl Popper, in his book *The Poverty of Historicism*,[1] gives us a whole catalogue of arguments against the scientific character and capacity of history, such as the impossibility of experimentation and quantification, the features of novelty, complexity, unpredictability, unavoidable selectivity of presentation, insufficiency of causal explanation, and so forth.

All such characteristics of history which make it unscientific, may, I believe, be derived from one essential difference in the foundations of history and science. Science is still based on the old assumption of the stability, immutability, and immovability of nature, which alone makes the establishment of "laws of nature" possible. Although the limitations of this assumption have recently begun to come into sight, the dimensional differences, spatial and temporal, between the human observer and the remotest moves of the forces of nature, the distances of human perspective, still make it possible and fruitful for human uses to act *as if* nature were stable. In fact, in human perspective nature *is* stable, its actual, fundamental changes and irregularities taking place in such gigantic and minuscule time-spaces, that they are irrelevant to human circumstances. On this basis of stable conditions, science can count on precisely quantifiable and accurately predictable regularities, it can establish "laws of nature," relatively, "statistically," valid as they may have shown to be on remote frontiers.

The human world, however, is ours; its changes and diversities are noticeable in our own familiar dimensions. We, human beings, have therefore come to experience and record them. In experiencing them, in being directly, communica-

[1] London, 1957, 2nd ed. 1960.

tively affected by them, we have developed that growing, ever more complex interrelation between our existence and our reflective capacities, which is history. The record of our accumulated experiences shows us variety and change, it implies irregularity and self-involvement, and the substance of this record does not lend itself to quantification and experimentation. So, in stark contrast with the domain of scientific research and methods, this world of human happening appears as an inexhaustible wealth of motley, chaotic, peculiar, and chance-propelled entities, among which people—and historians—move about with such patent delight. We learned, Geoffrey Barraclough states, "appreciation of the subtle shades of individuality, respect for irreducible particularity, acceptance of the untold 'multitude of facts,' and awareness of 'endless formation and transformation' . . . we see in history 'the most exhilarating testimony of the creative vigour, the splendid variety, of the human spirit.' "[2]

The strictly positivistic view of history is most sharply formulated by Karl Popper in his other book *The Open Society and Its Enemies:* "The realm of facts," he writes, "is infinitely rich, and . . . there must be selection. According to our interests, we could, for instance, write about the history of art; or of language; or of feeding habits; or of typhus fever . . . Certainly, none of these is the history of mankind (nor all of them taken together). What people have in mind when they speak of the history of mankind is, rather, the history of the Egyptian, Babylonian, Persian, Macedonian, and Roman empires, and so on, down to our own day. In other words: They speak about the *history of man-*

2 Geoffrey Barraclough, *History in a Changing World* (Norman, Okla., 1956), p. 2 (by permission of the publishers, The University of Oklahoma Press, 1956).

kind, but what they mean, and what they have learned about in school, is the *history of political power.* There is no history of mankind, there is only an indefinite number of histories of all kinds of aspects of human life. And one of these is the history of political power. This is elevated into the history of the world. But this, I hold, is an offence against every decent conception of mankind. It is hardly better than to treat the history of embezzlement or of robbery or of poisoning as the history of mankind. For *the history of power politics is nothing but the history of international crime and mass murder* (including, it is true, some of the attempts to suppress them)."[3]

So far, there is some undeniable truth in Professor Popper's statement. If the "history of mankind" were nothing else than this, that is, purely political history without any further implication—which, incidentally, has become for quite a time already a rather antiquated kind of historiography—Professor Popper would certainly be right in dismissing it as a futile pretension.

But, he continues, "is there really no such thing as a universal history in the sense of a concrete history of mankind? There can be none. This must be the reply of every humanitarian, I believe . . . A concrete history of mankind, if there were any, would have to be the history of all men. It would have to be the history of all human hopes, struggles, and sufferings. For there is no one man more important than any other. Clearly, this concrete history cannot be written. We must make abstractions, we must neglect, select. But with this we arrive at the many histories; and among them, at that history of international crime and mass murder

[3] Karl R. Popper, *The Open Society and Its Enemies,* new edition, (Princeton, 1963), vol. II, p. 270.

which has been advertised as the history of mankind." And the perfectly logical conclusion of these premises is that *"history has no meaning."*[4]

Now such a concept of "concrete" history, widespread among contemporary scholars, is indeed guilty of much "neglect" and, what is more important still, of a lack of clear distinctions, resulting from the belief in a democracy of facts. First of all, the organic species, Man, is more than the sum total of human beings—even a collective group of people is demonstrably more, or something else, than the sum total of its individuals. A nation is more than all of its nationals; residues of common life, common experiences and reflective responses to these experiences, traditions, institutions, achievements continuing effective, come in. And this complex of characteristics, forming a character, a "civilization," has a real existence of its own, it is no mere abstraction, or *"nomen."* So, in regard to any such national and civilizational entity, it cannot be said that "there is no one man more important than any other," as true as this certainly is in respect of human rights and dignity. Therefore, in regard to any history, be it the history of a nation, or that of any one of those functional histories which Professor Popper has in mind, certain men are undeniably more influential, indeed crucial, than other men. Newton and Einstein were doubtless more important for science than a multitude of physics professors, past and present.

Likewise, when we consider the history of humanity as a whole, there are eras, events, peoples, more influential than others, there are—and not by accident—certain peoples, personalities, processes, moving at certain times and places into the center of happenings and conspicuously determin-

[4] *Ibid.*

ing the currents of the epoch. Rome, I dare say, was more important than Phrygia, Augustine more important than Donatus of Carthage, Luther more important than Karlstadt. There are shifts of prominence from one country to another, from one kind of human activity and interest to another.

So the "subtle shades of individuality," the "creative vigour, the splendid variety, of the human spirit," the "infinite richness of the realm of facts" notwithstanding, there is, I contend, a definite order prevailing in human history, an order of a very special and many-dimensional kind. And order is the first prerequisite of meaning.

3

THERE ARE, FIRST OF ALL, DIFFERENT LEVELS OF history, which, in the current views of history are unnoticed or disregarded—therefore the realm of history must seem like a mere jumble of facts and phenomena, all equally valid, but immensely different in form and quality. "The appearance of irregularity in human history," Friedrich Schlegel says, "is produced only by the collision of heterogeneous spheres of Nature, which meet here and intermix."[1]

These levels of history correspond to different levels of human existence, for all of us human beings live at once on different levels: There is a physical level, and on that level, I am, with regard to my subordinate cells and organs, a genus and generality. There is the level of the individual person, on which I am, in relation to the superior entity, the community or collective to which I belong, an individual. There is the level of communities and collectives, of families, clans, tribes, nations, states, which, in turn, are, in relation to the "human race," particular, individual en-

[1] Athenaeumsfragment; Friedrich Schlegel, *Kritische Schriften* (München, 1938), p. 49.

tities. We may skip many intermediate levels, for instance—between individuals and their nation—institutions, organizations, collectives, working teams, etc.; and—between nations and the human race—cultural units or "civilizations." These levels coincide with different ranges of existential scope. Compare the range of the physical being, the animal, or the human being as animal, with the range of the completed person and his consciousness, or the range of a clan with the range of a nation, and the manifold implications of the enlargement of scope become evident.

When we survey the course of history, indeed of evolution, we cannot fail to notice the *gradual expansion of existential scope,* and certain events (often covering extended periods) which constitute caesuras, or turning points because their *center of gravity of existence shifts from one level to another level,* from a lower level with narrower scope to a higher level with wider scope. Such a caesura was for instance the evolutional transition from the animal to the human being.

The course of history shows a consecution of such shifts of existential points of gravity, of such degrees of existential and implicitly intellectual expansion of scope. This evolution—not to be confounded with progress, which has a moral, or merely functional connotation—proceeds from the tribe to the city and city-state, from the city-state, through the intermediary of feudal principalities, to the territorial estate, from the territorial estates to dynastical and nation-states, from nation-states to popular nations, from nations to civilizational and ideological power blocs, and finally to the technically, technologically prepared "one world" which is humanly, psychologically, very far from organized realization, but which looms as the only alternative

195

that science and technology have presented us to their opposite achievement, nuclear or biological annihilation.

Such existential shifts within the hierarchy of historical beings, and the attendant expansions of scope, include multifarious special developments: secularization, rationalization, scientification and technicalization, broadening of cosmic aspects, extension of physical and psychic insights, deepening and sensitizing of artistic faculties, transformation of consciousness, dynamization and acceleration of life; on all fronts of human endeavor an interchange and interaction takes place between the creation of new reality and the response to it.

This process, needless to say, does not involve an increase in morality. Morality is connected, indeed synonymous, with the awareness of human identity, and, therefore, man's responsibility toward and for his fellowmen. Such awareness and responsibility have, from their origins, been concentrated in personal consciousness, and never really in any group. It has therefore necessarily decreased with the increase of collectivity and depersonalization, with the emergence of a collective consciousness.

4

THIS CENTRAL, MANY-SIDED DEVELOPMENT, AS INDI-
cated in my "history of history," gives evidence of a definite
coherence. And what, in the domain of history, may be
considered the mode of order equivalent to science's laws
of nature, is what I would call *the rigor of coherence*. Historical coherence does not consist in simple causation, and
therefore the fundamental question of science *why* something is, or happens, does not apply to history. The historical
question is *how* it happened. When we start asking "why"
in history we are overwhelmed by so many, manifold, many-
level, and unfathomable causes, that causality melts into
conditionality, a conditionality that has no end.

This peculiarity of history, the unanswerable why, has to
do with the precarious and shifty nature of historical facts.
Causes lead from fact to fact. To be sure, there are certain
distinct facts in history which stand solidly by themselves.
It is possible to establish when a man was born or when he
died, when and where a battle was fought, or a decree was
issued. But such firmly established data, the only ones that
could compare with scientific facts, are devoid of causal

relation and acquire relevance only through connections with data of an entirely different order, data which do not stand firmly by themselves, but exist only in and through coherence with other data. This makes for considerable uncertainty. Since these data do not stand alone, but depend on manifold relations and circumstances, which cannot all be brought in evidence, they need to be structured by selection and supplemented by interpretation. There is now a wide agreement among historians that, whenever we touch upon something relevant to the understanding of a historical complex, we are compelled to interpretation. This is so, however, not only, as it is commonly stressed, because of the unreliability of documents and witnesses, or the mere "multitude of facts," but precisely because of the immense *coherence* of events and developments, in breadth and in depth.

Let us consider some examples on the more restricted, political level. Take the American Revolution. It is a stretched-out process. Does it start with the Declaration of Independence, or with the battle of Lexington, or with the Boston Tea Party? The Boston Tea Party refers us further back—and I skip a host of links—to the Townshend Act, the Stamp Act, the Colonial Currency Act, the Sugar Act, the writs of assistance. The Sugar Act was enacted by England for the purpose of raising revenues in the colonies, which were needed for defense and Indian administration, as a consequence of the acquisition of vast American territories from France. This acquisition, in turn, goes back to the French and Indian War, which was part of the Seven Years' War in Europe, and to the long, centuries-old colonial rivalry between Britain, France, and Spain. (In fact, the initial serious rift between England and the colonies developed from the colonies' trading with the enemy during the Seven Years' War.) Here we arrive at an altogether different scene of happenings. And so it goes on, leading us farther and farther back, through an ever broader, ever more complex genealogy of events, and this is only *one* line on *one* level of events. There are many lines, there are various levels. There is that higher, or deeper level: the traditions, mental attitudes, and habits that had grown apart in Britain and in the colonies. There are the colonial circumstances and problems. There is the individual level of the character, the social background, the psychology of George Washington and the men of the first congresses on the one hand, of the British statesmen and generals on the other.

What started the First World War? Was it the mobilization of Russia? The ultimatum of Austria? The assassination of the Archduke Francis Ferdinand? The Austrian annexation of Bosnia? The clash of the Hapsburg power interests with the Russian on the Balkans, which would have led to war much earlier, had Bismarck not restrained the hotheaded Crown Prince Rudolf? Was it the encirclement of Germany, as a result of the menacing expansion of the Reich, its army, navy, industry, colonial aspirations? Was it this rash overcompensation of an age-old German inferiority complex, the yearning for the long overdue realization of the missed hegemonial day; thus, the culmination of a millennial German predicament? Was it the mentality, representing this popular urge, of that romantically pompous upstart William II, or the carelessness of easygoing Count Berchtold, the irresponsibility of those Russian generals? Was it the brooding malaise of an obsolescent order? It was all of these taken together, converging on the disaster, coming far from the past and reaching far into the future.

199

The American Revolution and the First World War are but two prominent turning points. Whatever historical event we choose to consider, we shall find it, if we look closely enough, determined by a "multitude of causes," and these causes, on their part, are by no means isolated, sharply delimitable events. They are interrelated, they continually interact, they form complexes which are connected with other complexes. The term "cause" loses its sense in a flow of consistent conditioning. In fact, if we went far enough, we would find that everything is caused by everything. So whatever historical phenomenon we may contemplate, be it a people, a process, a happening, a personality, however selective we may have to proceed, our only chance to come close to understanding it is to study its complex coherence and historical continuity.

Nor is the *interaction of events* a simple matter. From Hegel (who followed Fichte) we have learned something very real, abstract and metaphysical as his system may be, namely the dialectical movement of history. We can recognize the full implications of this notion only when we strip it of the systematized and dogmatic guise which it was given by Hegel's disciples, particularly Karl Marx. Then we can see it effective throughout the course of history and in the most diverse forms, spatial and temporal. We have noticed the ambitendency in the advance of the idea of Progress, with recurrent regression actually furthering progression. We have observed in romanticism the interweaving, and in it the contraposition, of emotionalism and rationalism, the former driving the latter ahead. We have seen the idea of Progress engendering historism, and historism turning into historicism, thereby provoking the denial of history. In all times, especially those of actual revolution, we see action followed by reaction, and reaction radicalizing the action. Generations of different ages live together in the same period, reactionaries representing the past, and opposing the present and future. They have a real function, although we have to fight them. For, "to oppose," as Ambrose Bierce in his *Devil's Dictionary* rightly defines it, "is to assist with obstructions and objections."

The concept of a rigorous coherence of the process of history runs counter to present popular opinion—for reasons stated before—but also counter to current scholarly fashion. "The very concentration on development and continuity," Professor Barraclough writes, ". . . may well have been natural, and seemed well founded, a century ago; but today we are in a position to realize more clearly that such assumptions are at best partial views, and probably (more bluntly) deceptive half-truths. The historian who observed, over thirty years ago that 'continuity is by no means the most conspicuous feature of history' [F. J. C. Hearnshaw, 1921], put his finger unerringly on one central fallacy of historicism; and since that time we ourselves have experienced enough of discontinuity to feel renewed sympathy with all those historians who, from the time of Augustine and Orosius, have been more impressed by the cataclysmic than by the continuous in human affairs. Nor is it easy, any longer, to believe that 'the nature of anything is entirely comprehended in its development.' This plausible view leaves too little room for the impact of the fortuitous and the unforeseen, for the new, the dynamic and the revolutionary, which breaks through . . . untrammeled by the past, at every great turning-point in human history . . . no present-day issue is, or ever was, intelligible in terms of its history."[1]

[1] Geoffrey Barraclough, *History in a Changing World* (Norman, Okla., 1956), p. 4.

It is true that the nineteenth-century search for specific causal origins is obsolete, but, in my view, only to be superseded by a much more complex and comprehensive picture of historical coherence which includes what Professor Barraclough misses in the old one, the realization of the new, the dynamic, indeed the metahistorical. But it is a fallacy, and not even a half-truth that "the fortuitous . . . the new . . . the revolutionary . . . breaks through untrammeled by the past, at every great turning point in human history." There is no cataclysmic breakthrough in history which has not for a long time grown underground in very well known, discernible stages. Every one of the Western revolutions, the English, the French, the American, the Russian, were but the final results of manifold, clearly demonstrable, coherent preparations, some of them proceeding from a dim past. New, of course, is every stage of these preparations, but what makes them revolutionary, what makes them into turning points is the simultaneous outburst of the long assembled, latent forces and their conjunction which is always more than mere conglomeration. The simultaneous breaking forth itself changes the scene fundamentally. There was nothing fortuitous, or discontinuous in any of the historic cataclysms.

Nor has any religious and intellectual revolution, Christianity, the Reformation, the Renaissance, the Copernican, the Cartesian, the Newtonian revolutions, romanticism and expressionism, emerged without antecedents and gradual maturation. Even Nazism, unprecedented as its mechanized atrocities are, can be traced back to centuries of an unfortunate German history, indeed Luther; and its particular novelty consists in the relapse, in an age of technological and collectivistic methods, into an always latently or patently existent human bestiality. This certainly gives no comfort or satisfaction to someone who has lived through this period, but neither does it help to bring morality into the picture: morality could not be "pitchforked out of politics" —it has never been in it. Needless to say that understanding at which we are aiming is definitely *not* condoning.

5

THE PROPOSITION OF RIGOROUS HISTORICAL COHERENCE and continuity raises finally the crucial question of *determinism and the possibility of human freedom of choice, indeed human responsibility*. Sir Isaiah Berlin, although he has written a whole book about *Historical Inevitability*, treats this question, it seems to me, a little bit too lightly. "If the belief in freedom," he writes, "—which rests on the assumption that human beings do occasionally choose, and that their choices are not wholly accounted for by the kind of casual explanations which are accepted in, say, physics or biology—if this is a necessary illusion, it is so deep and so pervasive that it is not felt as such. No doubt we can try to convince ourselves that we are systematically deluded. But unless we attempt to think out the implications of this possibility, and alter our modes of thoughts and speech to allow for it accordingly, this hypothesis remains hollow; that is, we find it impossible even to entertain it seriously, if our behaviour is to be taken as evidence of what we cannot bring ourselves to believe or suppose not merely in theory, but in practice. My submission is that to make a serious attempt to adapt our thoughts and words to the hypothesis of determinism is scarcely feasible . . . The changes involved are too radical . . . We can, of course, work out the logical implications of any set of internally consistent premises—logic and mathematics will do any work that is required of them —but this is a very different thing from knowing how the result would look 'in practice,' what the concrete innovations are; and, since history is not a deductive science (and even sociology becomes progressively less intelligible as it loses touch with its empirical foundations), such hypotheses, being abstract models, pure and unapplied, will be of little use to students of human life. Hence the ancient controversy between free will and determinism, while it remains a genuine issue for theologians and philosophers, need not trouble the thoughts of those whose concern is with empirical matters— the actual lives of human beings in the space and time of normal experience. For historians determinism is not a serious issue."[1]

If I understand him correctly, Sir Isaiah implies that since it is impossible for us to live according to the assumption of determinism, we, "whose concern is with empirical matters" need not bother with the question at all. It seems to me, however, hardly permissible for anybody seriously concerned with empirical matters simply to ignore this fundamental question. It is indeed a serious, a fundamental issue, not only for the theologian and the philosopher, but for the historian as well, in fact, for every human being. Human life, "empirical matters," is not compartmentalized; if a philosopher, or a theologian takes his philosophy, or theology, really seriously, he has to relate what he is thinking and talking about to "empirical matters," i.e. to human life

[1] Isaiah Berlin, *Historical Inevitability* (London, New York, Toronto; 1954), pp. 33 f.

—otherwise what he is doing is not worth two cents. And so, a historian, whose concern is directly with empirical matters, has to bother all the more about a problem essential for the understanding of these matters. He is confronted with two alternatives: either to proceed "as if" determinism did not exist, that is, to follow the counsel of Vaihinger, or to come right out and deny the existence of determinism, which amounts to denying all historical coherence and continuity. I for one cannot bring myself to gloss over the issue of free will versus determinism with an "as if."

Fortunately, there is no either-or between determinism and free will. "The fact is," as Professor E. H. Carr states, "that all human actions are both free and determined, according to the point of view from which one considers them." In my interpretation of this fact, however, I am inclined to differ with Professor Carr, who, like Isaiah Berlin, sticks to the scientific pattern of plain causation. "Historians," he says, "frequently discuss alternative courses available to the actors in the story on the assumption that the option was open, though they go on quite correctly to explain why one course was eventually chosen rather than the other. Nothing in history is inevitable *except in the formal sense that, for it to happen otherwise, the antecedent causes would have had to be different.*"[2] This is, in fact, tantamount to admitting total inevitability, and thereby total determinism, the "formal sense" being strict causation, whereby Professor Carr contradicts his previous statement to which I adhere.

Human freedom, indeed exists, in spite of, and within historical coherence and continuity. It is in various ways

[2] Edward Hallett Carr, *What Is History?* (New York, 1962), pp. 124 ff. (Italics mine.)

built in, as it were, in the structure of coherence. Man has, in the course of a coherent evolution, acquired, extended, and developed the faculty of thinking—he has, in fact, developed it to a degree of specialistic perversion, as in the various forms of modern logic, which have an ultimately paralyzing effect. But essentially, and practically, thinking implies the faculty of choosing, and the feeling of freedom of choice. To be sure, unconscious, emotional, traditional, hereditary, environmental motivations come in as contributory factors determining reasoning and choice. But there is among these motivations a very profound and imponderable one, and that is, the immeasurable measure of vitality, of the vital power with which a person has been endowed by his whole organic constitution, a power effective in all the rest of his faculties, in his thinking, imagining, and acting. This is the wholly incommensurable factor in a person's experiences of life, this is what basically gives him the feeling of freedom. The depth of a man's vital power, and his momentary command over this power, its exuberant assertion or, conversely, its recessive diminution, may be decisive in critical situations. It may well have determined the character of historical events. Vitality is the driving force of imagination and will, and thus the element of human creation—and how can there be human creation without freedom? To be sure, the amount of vitality is also determined, but, being incommensurable, and not foreseeable from one moment to the other, it is an island of freedom in the flow of coherence. It is what cannot be accounted for precisely in the study of events and personalities.

I have submitted that human life, and so history, proceeds on different levels. There is the supreme level, the level of the evolution of man, the "history of history," which shows a coherence overarching the decisions of single men; there is, even on the apparently chaotic level of political life, an intrinsic evolutional coherence, noticeable in the expansion of scope, political and conceptual. In the coherence of such broad development a definite direction can be discerned—a direction, to be sure, without finality—which, when we view the whole coherence of happening, appears to exceed the power of human individuals—too much comes together, hangs together, converges, continually interacting and interreacting between levels, sections and regions of events, between the different ages, past, present, and future. So the *direction* happenings take has the character of inevitability and inescapability. The *ways,* however, in which things happen, appear to be subject to choices and decisions of individuals, to their thinking, and acting, and vital power. It was certainly no accident that the men who made the decisive steps were Paul, Augustine, Luther, or Copernicus, Galileo, Kepler, Newton, Einstein, and so forth, but it could have been other men, and they could have been brought to their achievements in other ways leading to the same results. And let us not forget that occasions, particular chances, and crucial moments are capable of favoring human creativity, of preparing the climate for it, of awakening, stirring the capacities of a person.

Accordingly, the trend of the whole process, the general direction in which events are moving, and the alternatives they are pointing to for choice and decision, can definitely be seen quite a distance ahead—in that respect the course of history is predictable. The particular ways it will take, the proportion of forces which will decide the grand issues, hiddenly determined as they themselves are, cannot be foreseen.

So determinism is by no means identical with fatalism. Determination by a variety of circumstances, among them evolutional coherence, need not and must not paralyze our will and feeling of freedom, and does not rid us of our human responsibility. We are not mere objects of a process, we belong to it, we are, with all our capacities, using our faculties to the full, part of the process, essential carriers of the process. To a high degree, our fortune, our chance, depends on whether we think and act in the direction of changing reality; and not only our personal destiny depends on it, but, what is much more important, the ways of human destiny, which are our responsibility. In point of fact, if this responsibility is our serious concern, it runs counter, more often than not, to our momentary personal opportunities.

6

MEANING, WE HAVE SEEN, IS ESSENTIALLY ORDER, coherence, unity of diversities, as conceived by a comprehending mind, i.e. by a consciousness. The fact that a unity of diversities is conceived, in itself creates order and coherence, which is meaning. I have distinguished two kinds of meaning: an external kind that connects one entity with others, that constitutes an aiming of somebody at some end beyond himself, or the serving of something as an instrument for something else—this is *meaning as purpose;* and another, internal kind, representing unity of diversity *within* a phenomenon, or process, a coordination of parts within a structural order—*meaning as form.*

In history, we have seen meaning as a goal, which for ages guided human beings in the conduct of their lives, fading away along with the expectation of the advent of a Kingdom of God, and eventually passing over into the hope for a final blessed state of humanity as the result of secular Progress. But even this hope has vanished. Indeed, the last movement to raise such expectancy, the Marxist, has begun to understand, that life, by its very nature, can have no finite goal, that it moves, transcends itself perpetually, that it *consists* of movement and self-transcendence and the tensions which this involves. The bliss in the beyond and the millennium here below are a gilding of death. Finality is at an end.

So for many people, including scholars and thinkers, who plainly identify meaning with a finite aim, history has no meaning. And with it life has ceased to have meaning: it is a mere point of existence, binding past and future in a precarious present and what there may be of meaning is "invented" by us.

There is, however, I contend, a meaning inherent in form, the meaning as coherence of happening, evolutional coherence. Not only the rounded lives and characters of personalities, works, nations, processes display it, but history as a whole shows such inner coherence. Persons are mortal, nations and civilizations are mortal, glorifying immortalizations notwithstanding. Their very forms imply birth and death. Viewing our present human situation, we have to ask ourselves where we stand, where history stands.

In the course of history we find, on the one hand, a definite, incontestable advance in the expansion of the inner and outer scope of existence. On the other hand—and this has disturbed the most progressive minds—important peoples and civilizations have declined and fallen, and even the evolutional movement advances in a temporal dialectic of action and reaction, ebbs and floods, recessions for further advances, in short, rotational moves. In the seventeenth century, a progressive divine, George Hakewill, noticing the growth, fading, and stronger reflourishing of learning and the arts from one people to another, called this "a kind of circular progress." From our present vantage point, history

211

appears as a *circular expansion,* a spiral advance, blending particularity with generality. But in this process the general is so completely one with the particular that it cannot be abstracted in the scientific way without undoing the very nature of the phenomenon.

The Greeks had not arrived at a true realization of the uniqueness of the historical process, while the opposite Judaeo-Christian concept, of which the idea of Progress was the secular heir, emphasized the uniqueness of human destiny. At the end of the nineteenth century, *Nietzsche,* violently reacting against historicism, found meaning and comfort in the concept of eternal recurrence, but in our thoroughly secular age, such a concept was bound to differ fundamentally from its Greek prototype: the background of divinity, the solid ground of divine eternity, on which that recurrence of the ancients had moved, had rested in moving, is gone. Nietzsche's recurrence moves in the void, it is sheer rotation as such.

Nietzsche's contemporary, *Jacob Burckhardt,* in like temper anticipated later interpretations. In his *Weltgeschichtliche Betrachtungen* (Reflections on World History) he rejected all "philosophy of history," under which term he understood all attempts at viewing human history as a whole. In opposition to such attempts he tried to discover general laws of history—not in an explicitly scientific sense, but rather loosely, tentatively, in a more impressionistic fashion. His firm rooting in the old traditions and values, and his great historical sensibility prevented him from a strict emulation of science, and from the rash and excessive interpretations, in which more recent theorists have indulged. On the other hand, in his *Kultur der Renaissance* (Culture of the Renaissance) and in his lectures on the History of Greek Culture a new sense of the organic wholeness and peculiarity of a historical epoch, or entity, manifested itself, exhibiting meaning as form. Both of these trends, however, the quasi-scientific concern with the general and the concern with the unique, appeared side by side, theoretically unconnected with each other. And for him, no less than for Nietzsche, history had lost its coherence and continuity; history in its proper sense had ceased to exist.

These ideas, at the time when they were issued, went almost unnoticed by the broad public. The world-shaking and value-shaking catastrophe of the First World War was needed to prepare the ground for their thriving and widespread influence. The man of the hour was *Spengler,* proclaiming the "Decline of the West." In his theory the various trends meet, that of Nietzsche and those of Burckhardt. He uses the idea of eternal recurrence to search for general laws of history. But other views, which had emerged in the meantime, stressing the organic and unique mingled with this search for general laws. Spengler is, in fact, the true exponent of the transitional and very confused intellectual situation of the 1920's. The aims of science are combined with residues of the philosophies of Dilthey and Bergson, with new vitalistic and holistic trends in the biology, palaeobiology, and anthropology of the time, the ideas of men like Driesch, Oskar Hertwig, Jakob von Uexküll, Leo Frobenius, scientists who developed the notion of the complex interrelations within the organic being and between the inner structure of a species and its specific environment. Spengler's theory is a blend of all these tendencies. History is broken up into incoherent parts, distinct cultures which rise and decline like any organic being, and, in rising and falling, go through definite stages, common to all of them, and

213

therefore explorable and predictable like physical regularities. It is, in fact, a return to parochial history in the Greek sense, but since our world experience has grown larger than that of the Greeks, it is now several parochial histories instead of one. Each of these disconnected cultures has a world of its own: not only does it grow from particular natural surroundings, but it reflects its inner and outer world in particular attitudes and responses, customs and outlooks, styles of arts and of sciences. No relation is established between the two aspects of this concept, that of the generalities, the "laws of history," and that of the singularities, the special characteristics of the various cultures.

Toynbee, a brilliant author and a more solid, but less imaginative scholar than Spengler, whose disciple he is, covers his far greater number of "philosophically contemporaneous" global civilizations with a superstructure of religious progress which, however, has only tenuous and indistinct connections with those civilizations. Unlike Spengler, more like Vico at the turn of the seventeenth century, he leaves to man a certain amount of freedom to influence his destiny with the help of divine guidance. To Toynbee, the "divine plan," as he calls Vico's "Providence," seems to be active in the laws of history, by stirring man to religious progress, to an ever "farther advance toward communion with God," by teaching man through suffering, and making him susceptible to a "cumulative increase in the means of Grace." "If religion is a chariot," Toynbee says in his essay on *Christianity and Civilization,* "it looks as if the movement of civilizations may be cyclic and recurrent, while the movement of religion may be on a single continuous line." This is a statement of faith with which one cannot and should not argue.

214

7

IN GENERAL, AS THE VARIOUS TESTIMONIES OF THE HIStorians of our days show, a tendency toward the acceptance of historical discontinuity and return to the old cyclic and cataclysmic theories continues to prevail. In none of the modern theories, as far as they are known to me, has the cyclic movement been established as the very medium of evolutional coherence, in none of them is history seen as *cyclic expansion.*

If we may assume that the view of history as cyclic expansion is valid, in what stage, at what point of this process do we find ourselves today? What is the meaning of our moment within the meaning of history?

In our present situation *two paradoxical features* stand out: For the first time *the human world is technically one, but at the same time in a state of wildest anarchy.* And *Western civilization is about to conquer the globe* and gradually extirpate the old customs, the peculiar cultural heritage of other peoples, while *the West at home, in its own domain, shows unmistakeable signs of degeneration.*

These two paradoxes are somehow related. Modern tech-

215

nology, the product and achievement of Western civilization, has functionally contracted the world into a single unit, not only extrinsically, by its various instruments of mass communication, but also intrinsically, by spreading everywhere its daily proliferating machinery of life-preservation and life-destruction, of comforts and atrocities, which will soon be the common property of a standardized world. So the technical developments change human conditions, and even the very foundations of human life. But man, human individuals and established communities do not keep pace with these rapid changes. This is easily understandable: Organic processes, psychic processes, are slow, having to overcome inertia, habits, traditions and inhibitions of all kinds; they need time, their natural time, their historical time of action and reaction, advance and recession. But mechanical developments, especially when a whole civilization sets all its pride and energy in their promotion, proceed quite unimpeded, in an almost automatic consecution. Our whole modern apparatus of human existence, including the apparatus of ideologies, took on dimensions appropriate only to vast collective units. But man, in his aspirations and volitions, has remained a narrow, however nationally inflated, self. The discrepancy, the clash, and the interaction of these two tendencies have brought about the present, unprecedented anarchy. It is unprecedented precisely because it comes into friction with, and is, on the other hand, functionally aided by, the technical unity. The political world has always been anarchical, but today for the first time, this anarchy surges against a technical counterforce.

The second paradox consists in the ambivalent role of Western civilization. This Western civilization represents, Toynbee notwithstanding, the leading strain of human evolution, and only the present outright denial of evolution permits our intellectuals to dispute this fact. Toynbee's great contribution was to draw attention to the vast variety of cultures and historical phenomena which have been neglected by previous considerations of history, and to comprehend in his view the new revelations of archaeology and ethnology. This widening of our vision has, however, by no means invalidated the evolutionally leading role of the Western branch of humanity, a statement which should not be interpreted as a disparaging of those other cultures. They are equal in stature, but not in evolutional importance, an importance which, from a human point of view, may be considered of questionable worth. But the sheer evidence tells us, that, in comparison with Western civilizational reach, regarding both intellectual and territorial expansion, the other, indigenous cultures must appear in some degree "retarded" or "arrested." Directly, or indirectly, they receive their up-to-date training from the West.

Any satisfaction, however, the West may derive from such evolutional superiority must be strongly tempered when we turn to the inner condition of this civilization. Let us, again, leave aside moral considerations which have come to be looked down upon as naively anachronistic and are officially regarded, more or less avowedly, as an undue interference in public affairs, especially when it comes to devising the extermination in a few minutes of hundreds of millions of human beings. On our globe there still exist evolutionally retarded peoples—peoples at least, not governments—which in their preservation of human dignity and propriety by far outrank the Western nations.

Other ominous symptoms may be seen among us. The most formidable achievements of Western man are certainly those in science which has penetrated and keeps incessantly advancing into zone after zone of our universe, and into the depths of organic and inorganic structures. Western, Western-informed, man has indeed eaten from the tree of life, but by doing this he appears to have eaten away his own substance, his inmost life. His very "making" threatens to kill him. I have indicated earlier the immense, uncontrolled growth of an impersonal, collective consciousness in sciences, institutions, bureaucracies, and so forth, and a correlative shrinking of the personal consciousness of individuals. This results in the people's waxing incapacity to control its government, and opens the way for the usurpation of power by extralegal collective forces. Electrical brains seize more and more of what had been the work of human hands and the creative ground of human minds. The unchannelled overrationalization of our life compresses the unconscious which bursts out into neuroses and follies of all kinds, and manifests its growing prevalence in wholly directionless, inarticulate performances like "action painting" and "pop art." And in the midst of the inanity of luxuriant luxuries, of apathy, routine, ennui, we find artistic creations of desolate beauty picturing the grotesque contrasts of our incoherent world, and conveying the tragic failure of human communication in an age of accomplished functional media. It is, all in all, an uncanny sight, reminiscent of the Roman Empire at the moment of its greatest expanse, a situation which seems to suggest that the life cycle of the West is approaching its end.

Our engineers of destruction have ventured to trace in the minutest details the course and the consequences of nuclear war. They have begun to "think the unthinkable," which unfortunately makes it appear thinkable, though this it never can be, however rationally accurate the prognosis of instances. Even apart from inevitable oversights, what cannot be calculated is the ever-intensifying chain interaction of happenings and circumstances which constitutes a real process. However, given the blind, obdurate ideological struggle with its mad "security" race, the ultimate conflagration as such is a conceivable possibility. In this case, the survival of Western civilization, in its indigenous, not transmitted, form, appears rather unlikely. This is not a matter of numbers, statistics, and machines. It is a matter of vital resources making peoples capable of sustaining the great transformations which are bound to follow in the wake of such a cataclysm. The Slavs, and particularly the colored peoples of Asia and Africa, seem to have far better chances, not so much because of their overpowering millions, but because of their basic human substance, which is not so spent as ours. The long dormant vital power of their masses, awakened and trained by Western methods, may—perhaps after a new "dark age"—take up the torch and carry it further.

This is one alternative. The other one would be that we, the West, join forces with these peoples of the future, regardless of ideologies and leanings, and that we, all together, realize what potentially exists already, an organized, supranational world order. This would mean the completed rounding of the cycle which began at the source of that Western civilization now shaping the population of the earth. It would confirm the meaning of *history as form;* at the same time it is a *goal,* however transient. If it could be reached, this again would not be anything final, not a millennium to repose in. Tensions would go on, problems would go on, for life would go on—and this, the *salvation of human life,* the *preservation of the human form is itself the true goal.* The overpopulation of our globe, this most disturbing common problem of humanity, may force men to migrate and found colonies on other habitable planets—the present search for interstellar communication seems to point that way. A new cycle may begin. All this appears imaginary today, as unthinkable as the other, sinister alternative, but this, the positive outlook, would be worth making thinkable, as thinkable as possible. It would demand as a prerequisite an effort at integration, not only political and racial, but also intellectual integration, control of our masterless collective consciousness. Our task, indeed our *foremost duty* is, it seems to me, to search for, apart from and above all specialized studies, the essential meaning of what we are doing, where it leads to, and what we achieve or produce by it; to seek what we have lost, an orientation in our world and the direction in which we should move.

The problem of the meaning of history is the problem of the meaning of man, the problem of a meaning of human life. We stand at the crossroad between the annihilation of the West and the unification of humanity. This is the time, if ever there was one, to raise fundamental questions.

Index

221